THE NEW COMPLETE

Scottish Terrier

by JOHN T. MARVIN

SECOND EDITION

1986—Second Printing

HOWELL BOOK HOUSE Inc.

230 Park Avenue

New York, N.Y. 10169

A famous pair: Harry Lauder and the
great Ch. Heather Realisation, 1936.

Courtesy, *Dog News*

Library of Congress Cataloging in Publication Data

Marvin, John T.
    The new complete scottish terrier.

      Rev. ed of : The complete scottish terrier. 1967.
      Bibliography: p. 255
      1. Scottish terriers. I. Title.
SF429.S4M3   1981   636.7'55   81-13416
ISBN 0-87605-306-1   AACR2

To my
Grandchildren,
Gretchen, Charlie and John
all lovers of
dogs

The Dog and his Shadow, Landseer, 1826.

Contents

A Landseer vignette, 1824. Note old type of Terrier at the left.

Foreword

If a man has once owned a Scottie, he will never want to own any other dog.
— F. W. Barton

As A LOVER of all Terrier breeds and especially those of Scottish descent, it was a rare privilege to write this book. The research involved in assembling the information contained between these covers was a pleasant experience since it brought me into close contact with many people interested in and dedicated to the Scottish Terrier.

I have endeavored to trace the history of the breed from the early beginnings of the domesticated dog through the derivation of the Terrier breeds and into the development of the Scottish Terrier as we know it today. I have mentioned many names in the chronological exposition of the breed but space limits their number. I had to concentrate on those persons and dogs that, in my opinion, were the most important in the Scottish Terrier's long, interesting narrative. I hope that all will understand and accept my position.

This, the updated version of *The Complete Scottish Terrier*, has offered me the opportunity to modify portions of the original effort, to improve upon the accuracy of statements made and to add much of historical interest that has been discovered since publication of the first edition. Also, of substantial interest to devotees of the breed, is the addition of numerous illustrations showing early dogs that had an impact on the breed; reproductions of paintings and prints illustrating the Scotsman and tableaux of noteworthy dogs, handlers and owners of yesteryear. All these early illustrations together with much

7

additional current material, offers interested readers deeper knowledge with which to extend their understanding of the Scot and its derivation.

At this time, I wish to thank my friends and correspondents in Canada, Great Britain and the United States who have so graciously supplied me with data and photographs that have helped make this edition more interesting and complete. I wish to offer specific thanks to Miss Barbara Kingsbury and R. Stephen Shaw for their efforts in making available to me invaluable photographs and information from the files of Barberry Knowe Kennels. My long-time friend, John W. Hillman supplied me with many photographs, stud cards, letters and memories dating back into the twenties. All this material and information has added great value to this revised effort.

Of course, a major addition to the new edition is the expansion of contemporary breed history. This includes biographies of fanciers and their dogs' accomplishments that became prominent in the breed since the first edition bowed in 1967, together with help in elaborating upon other material noted previously. It is hoped that the information presented herein is both accurate and in proper chronological order, any errors are both unintentional and regretted. The very immensity of the task together with the ever-changing ownership of many of the dogs involved lends the opportunity for error. I trust that each of you will derive as much pleasure reading this effort as I have gained in revising it.

JOHN T. MARVIN

Scotch Terrier, 1840.

1

Introducing the Scot

"ALL dogs are good; any Terrier is better; a Scottish Terrier is the best." So said William Haynes many years ago. Today, no fancier of the Scotsman will disagree, which proves that the statement is still true and that the breed attributes have been maintained throughout the intervening years. This love of the strain may be traced directly to its character. This is not a superficial breed or one with lavish tongue and a quick-to-forget approach. Rather, the Scot is a bit on the dour side, as might be expected from his heritage, sometimes solemn but always loyal to his master. The Scottish Terrier is dignified, slow to react and show affection, and steadfast whatever the circumstance.

The Scot melds the virtues prudence, enthusiasm, stability and selective affection into every act of his small body and vital life. These qualities are cherished by those who understand him and by his master most of all, for he *is* his master's dog. In this respect I can sa *r* without fear of contradiction that there never was a promiscuous Scottie, or one that loved everybody. Many of the breed will tolerate others, particularly when these persons have their master's blessing. But for absolute adoration concentrated upon one or two people, the Scot has no rival, which is why his following is legion and loyal.

S.S. Van Dine (pen name of Willard Huntington Wright) a noted novelist and himself a Scottie devotee and breeder once wrote:

> A quality of the Scottie is his aloofness. He has a sense of bashfulness, and despite his vigorous nature, he is highly sensitive. Like all well-bred people he hates to be stared at. If you look straight at him in a critical way he will turn his head and attempt to act indifferently. He dislikes to have his privacy invaded and, like any gentleman, resents being the centre of attraction.

Lest some may think the breed lacks sparkle, let it be said that Scotties will play as any other dog; they will chase a ball, plunge in a lake for a swim and in general act like all Terriers. But their attachment to their master and his family is different and more profound than with most dogs. This difference is the major quality that draws and holds so many to this small and intense breed.

The Scottish Terrier is a wary dog that will observe a provocative situation with smoldering and often averted eyes and without evidence of any great interest. What is he thinking? Why does he suddenly decide to enter the fray with enthusiasm? I believe it is because the Scottie, like his human counterpart, is a canny indi-

A typical litter by Ch. Heather Fashion Hint ex Walnut Carmine, owned by Mr. and Mrs. Morris Yowell.

10

vidual that never acts without reflection and consideration of the consequences. Once the decision is made, however, he enters the melee with authority and abandon.

A compilation of compliments paid to this breed by its many admirers would fill volumes. Two of the most revealing of these add insight into its basic character. The first was written by S. S. Van Dine:

> A Scottie's character is hard to analyze, as are all colorful personalities; and it may perhaps best be described as an ever-blazing internal fire, both physical and tempermental that shines forth from his eyes, vitalizes his expression, invigorates his body and animates his activity.

Dorothy Gabriel wrote:

> The character of the Scottish Terrier is wonderful. He is essentially a one-man's dogs, loving his home and owner and having absolutely no use for outsiders. He never forgets — his heart will break with grief, but he will not yowl about it. He is absolutely honorable, incapable of a mean or petty action, large hearted and loving with the soul and mind of an honest gentleman.

These tributes sum up the many fine qualities of the Scottie, and they may constitute the reason why the late Vinton Breese said: "Once a Scot owner, always a Scot owner, for no other breed can fill his unique place."

"Puffin Shooting." Lithograph after T. M. Baynes, circa 1830. This very rare print of an unusual sport includes typical highland dogs of the period. These ranged in color from black to white and were selected for on the basis of working quality alone.

A group of terriers of the 1860s including three of Scottish heritage. The dog at the extreme left is probably an early Scotch Terrier. A Westie is seen in the left foreground facing a dog of Dandie Dinmont stamp. The others are a Manchester, a Fox Terrier and a Bull Terrier.

2

The Background and Heritage of the Terrier Family

Volumes have been written concerning the dog, its origin and habits. This book, while being directed primarily to the Scottish Terrier will, in this chapter, delineate a helpful working background for the novice while serving to refresh the memories of more serious fanciers in matters of general interest.

The basic genealogy of the dog is completely obscured in the dimness of the past. Undoubtedly, all breeds of dog descended from common ancestors and these same ancestors were probably those of the wolf.* The osteology of the wolf is similar to that of the dog, and the wolf and dog cohabit freely, lending credence to the claim of descent from the same progenitors.

The Shepherd's dog is sometimes credited as the dog most nearly approaching the primitive race and the dog from which the Terrier

*Youatt On The Dog, 1845

descended through the Hound, as set forth in the Genealogical Table of Buffon.† In his book, *Rural Sports*, Daniel agrees that cohabitation between the wolf and the dog does occur and that hybrids of varying degrees of ferocity are produced, as evidenced by the early Siberian dogs. He doubts, however, that any wolf blood flows in the veins of the truly domesticated dog.

Regardless of its origin, the dog has been known to man for as long as records have been kept. The Bible refers to them more than forty times in the Old and New Testaments.* Figures of dogs and dog-like deities have been found carved in relief on ancient works of stone, the earliest being on the Tomb of Amten in Egypt, which dates back to the Fourth Dynasty, or between 3500 and 4000 B.C. Appreciation of a dog's fidelity led the early Egyptians to apply the designation of "Dog Star" to Sirius. This, the brightest star in the heavens, always appeared as a forerunner to the periodic floods of the river Nile, and was a signal for the shepherds to move their flocks to higher ground. Its appearance was so reliable that these simple people believed it to be a symbol of watchfulness and fidelity and, hence, named it after the dog, who was always held in great veneration by the ancient tribes of the Pharaohs. In old Roman dwellings, a chained dog was often depicted on the mosaic threshold with the accompanying words *Cave Canem* (beware of the dog). The early Europeans used the dog as a symbol of fidelity and loyalty. Ecclesiastical representations of holy patrons are replete with dogs; Saint Benignus has a dog by his side; Saint Bernard is shown with a dog at his feet; and Saint Sira is pictured with dogs about her. From earliest history, dogs have been the protectors of the habitation of man. In every age and in all parts of the globe, dogs have played an important part in the labors and sports of men, sharing trial, danger, and pleasure with equal zeal.

> The poor dog in life, the firmest friend,
> The first to welcome, foremost to defend:
> Whose honest heart is still his master's own,
> Who labours, fights, lives, breathes for him alone.
>
> — Byron

Throughout centuries of civilization, canines have been the true and constant friends of the human race. They have full and

The Complete Dog Book, 1975.
†*Rural Sports,* by Daniel, 1802.

14

Cave Canem. Beware of the Dog. From a mosaic at Pompeii.

unequalled respect for persons of all creeds, races, and stations of life, asking only a little praise and affection in payment for their unfailing devotion. In short, the steadfastness and fidelity of the dog is unmatched by any other member of the animal world.

> With eye upraised, his master's looks to scan,
> The joy of solace, and the aid of man;
> The rich man's guardian, and the poor man's friend,
> The only creature, faithful to the end.
>
> —Crabbe

Other domesticated animals submit to human control but rarely do they recognize their master except in connection with the supplying of their wants. A dog, on the other hand, will starve with its master and suffer any hardship or indignity in order to be close to the object of its affection. Many dogs have been known to grieve over the loss of their masters to the extent of refusing food and drink and finally dying of broken hearts—where can one find greater love?

Early concepts of the utilitarian advantages of the dog varied little from today's views. Dogs have been used as drovers, dray animals, hunters, vermin destroyers, and companions. Today, their use differs not at all; we probably stress their companionship to a greater degree, but the canine still has the same definite uses to which ends it exerts its every effort. The advent of police, guard, and guide work has even extended the field of purposeful existence that has always been that of man's best friend.

To obtain a better insight into the canine race, the zoological ranking and biological background of the animal will be of interest. The dog belongs to that division of quadrapeds termed *vertebrata*, and it ranks in the class *mammalia* because the female suckles her young. It is of the tribe *unguiculata*, since it is armed with nails or claws which are not retractile, and is of the order of *digitigrades* because it walks on its toes. The dog is of the genus *canis*, in view of its tooth arrangement, and belongs to the sub-genus *familiaris* by reason of the round shape of the pupil of its eye, which distinguishes it from the wolf, fox, and jackal, all of which stem from the same genus.

Members of the genus *canis* are basically carnivorous animals; that is, they are primarily meat eaters. The dog is equipped for such

16

a diet with an excellent set of forty-two teeth, including twelve incisors (small front teeth) that are adapted for cutting and seizing; four canines (the long pointed tusk-like dentition) which are for tearing, stabbing, or for "fixing" the struggling prey; and twenty-six premolars and molars (the broader, heavy rear teeth having substantially flat complex crowns) that are used as grinders for crushing food. The milk dentition, or first teeth (puppy teeth), are fewer in number, since certain of the molars and premolars have no predecessors. In general, the permanent teeth begin to replace the puppy teeth at about four months of age.

The dog tears its food and often bolts large pieces with little or no mastication. The stomach is of simple structure capable of digesting this unchewed food, and the intestines are of length medium between the short ones of the true *carnivora* and the long ones of *graminivorous* animals. For these reasons, dogs can easily digest diverse foods, including grains and vegetables in addition to meat and, therefore, thrive on mixed diets.

From the beginning of the recorded history of the dog, different breeds or strains have been known. Dogs have for centuries been selectively bred by man for the purpose at hand. As the need for a different type arose, that type was bred. Bird dogs, sight and scent Hounds, workers, fighters, and Terriers are but a few of the many special types that have been bred.

Since dogs are tractable and easily trained for almost any purpose, it has been a relatively easy task to modify and change characteristics of a breed or variety and by selection and cross-breeding to obtain the type of animal desired. This statement is readily proved by the fact that in 1873 only forty breeds and varieties were known, whereas today some 300 breeds and varieties are recognized throughout the world.

All modern breeds of dogs are hybrids — crosses of various breeds and strains to obtain the desired characteristics. When these crosses, through selection and several generations of reproduction, breed true, the characteristics of the breed may be termed "set" and a new breed is established. Today's 125 recognized distinct breeds (1982) of dogs have all attained this station. They are "set" in their characteristics and conformation. Occasional throwbacks occur, but the great majority of their progeny breed reasonably true to type.

The British Isles was the birthplace of that grouping of dogs known as "Terriers" and in this family of canines belongs our distinguished Scots. Terriers, as evidenced by their Group name (derived from the Latin, "Terra," meaning earth), are all earth dogs, going to ground after their prey. They are of special temperament, have high intelligence and unquestioned courage. They will fight to the death rather than yield ground or give quarter. And, above all, they respect man.

An interesting description of a "Terrier" was written in 1774 by Oliver Goldsmith, who said: "The terrier is a small kind of hound, with rough hair, made use of to force the fox and badger out of their holes; or rather to give notice by their barking, in what part of their kennel the fox or badger resides, when the sportsmen intend to dig them out."

This description calls for the Terrier to be a barking dog, one bred not only to fight the fox and badger, etc., but also "to give notice" where they reside. Thus, the Terrier, when he went to ground, was expected to bark constantly to tell the hunter where he was going so that the earth could be dug and the prize captured and killed. Sportsmen for many years have had little care for a Terrier without "good voice," and one who is so deficient is no Terrier at all. For these reasons, we can expect today's Terrier to enjoy a lusty bark when conditions demand; it is his heritage.

A very early reference* suggests that a good breed of "Terrier" comes from "a Beagle and a mongrel Mastiff, or from any small thick-skinned dog that had courage..." These Terriers presumably did not have good voice, and a "collar of bells" was placed around their necks to give notice of direction and to cause the fox to leave his den. This reference is interesting but is not in agreement with opinions of many other authorities who seemingly concur on the antiquity and qualities of the Terrier.

The exact origin of the basic Terrier blood is so obscure that it discourages conjecture. Early writers on dogs refer to any earth dog as a Terrier, as noted above, and German scientists have written for many years of short-legged, generally long-backed dogs under the generic term "Basset." This grouping has included Dachsunds, Basset Hounds and "Terriers." The basis for this grouping and its true

*Rural Sports, by Daniel, 1802

18

Scotch Terriers (1835, by Smith)

"Waiting" or sometimes called "Highland Dogs," circa 1839 by Landseer' showing
a Highland Terrier in the foreground.

interpretation are not known, although the general outline of the breeds in question lends some right to the belief that all these short-legged breeds were derived from common basic blood.

The development of the distinct breeds and strains known today was the result of purposeful breeding techniques practiced by early breeders who carefully chose the parents and selected only the best of the "get" for reproductive purposes. The young dogs were trained for the work and the most adept and biddable were again bred, with careful selection, to assure courage and determination. As time progressed, crosses with other breeds were introduced to yield special characteristics indigenous to those breeds. Among the Terriers, the Hound was used to increase keenness of scent and improve disposition. Crosses with fighting dog breeds were introduced to intensify tenacity and increase courage. In fact, the several Terrier breeds include many infusions which yielded for their wise breeders the types of dogs desired.

As their name implies, Terriers were originally bred to destroy ground animals, and, for this pursuit, they are still adept. They kill rats, foxes, otters, badgers, and all other vermin that have the temerity to cross their path. Larger breeds of Terriers will fight it out with anything on four legs, and the Airedale has been used successfully to hunt mountain lion and bear.*

As time went on, different sections of the country, different towns, and even different large estates developed distinct strains of the more basic Terrier breeds which best suited their limited purpose. From these strains come our present day Terrier breeds.

A listing of the related dogs in the Terrier Group (Group IV) as recognized by the American Kennel Club (1982) is as follows:

Airedale Terrier
American Staffordshire Terrier
Australian Terrier
Bedlington Terrier
Border Terrier
Bull Terrier (White)
Bull Terrier (Colored)
Cairn Terrier
Dandie Dinmont Terrier

*All About Airedales, R.M. Palmer, 1911

20

Fox Terrier (Wire)
Fox Terrier (Smooth)
Irish Terrier
Kerry Blue Terrier
Lakeland Terrier
Manchester Terrier
Miniature Schnauzer
Norfolk Terrier
Norwich Terrier
Scottish Terrier
Sealyham Terrier
Skye Terrier
Soft-Coated Wheaten Terrier
Staffordshire Bull Terrier
Welsh Terrier
West Highland White Terrier

All members of the Terrier family have the instinctive desire to enjoy a good frolic or a fight. This should not be taken as a condemnation that all Terriers are fighters; they are not. Some Terriers will be less argumentative than others. However, no Terrier has ever been known to back away from a fight or act the coward—it is just not breed character. In fact, the courage indigenous to all Terrier breeds can best be traced to early training and environment. It has been retold many times that "keepers" of kennels for the Scotch gentry would test the young dogs for gameness. This test frequently consisted of dropping the dog into an upended barrel in which a young badger, or other equally ferocious foe, was waiting. If the dog killed or mortally wounded his adversary, he was considered a worthy addition to the pack. If not, few tears were shed.

This method of determining gameness seems "extreme" today, but it was a realistic approach in the days when the main purpose of the Terrier was to rout out or kill the game in its earth. It is also the reason why today's Terriers are so fearless, for with the test outlined above, few that were not game survived to father descendants.

In spite of this early training, Terriers are proud, friendly, affectionate, and intelligent. They make wonderful pets and companions, and few who have ever owned a Terrier will consider any other breed as a replacement when that sad need arises in their lives.

Vignette of early terriers from Sydenham Edwards' *Cynographia Britannica*, circa 1801.

3

The Scotch and the Scottish Terrier

As NOTED in Chapter 2, most authors before 1800 agreed that there were two varieties of the Terrier but none offered definitive names for them. Long-legged and short-legged they remained, and in short and long coats of many colors. This indicates that early Terriers were not always of pure blood but historically there is evidence of pure ancestry at that time.

With the coming of the 19th century, sportsmen and others became increasingly aware of the need for special abilities in dogs and because of this began to reproduce such animals by breeding techniques that progressed with each passing year. The Terriers were separated into strains which later became distinct breeds each with a conformation and temperament that was tailored for a given purpose.

The fact that the original Terrier variants were bred in specific areas and localities was not mentioned in most early sporting books. This was to be expected, for the majority of the authors were not dog men but sportsmen who knew that dogs existed but who cared not for their derivation. The flood of dog books of the early 19th century attempted to explain the origin and conformation of the several varieties known at the time. *Cynographica Britannica* by Sydenham Edwards (*circa* 1800) was the first of these. This was issued in quarterly sections but never completed. Nevertheless, the colored plate of Terriers together with a description thereof offers some interesting information. Five widely different varieties of Terriers are depicted. The Manchester or Black and Tan is easily identifiable. The rather typical Scotch Terrier is of a reddish wheaten color. This plate proves there were several different Terrier breeds in 1800, and it suggests that earlier authors neglected to give proper descriptions of them. Thomas Brown in his *Biographical Sketches and Authentic Anecdotes of Dogs* (1829) made a great contribution to the study of the Terrier breeds. Here the student finds the first real breakdown of the Terrier kind. Brown said:

> There are two kinds of Terriers, — the rough haired Scotch and the smooth English.
> The Scotch terrier is certainly the purest in point of breed and the English seems to have been produced by a cross from him. The Scotch terrier is generally low in stature, seldom more than twelve or fourteen inches in height, with a strong, muscular body, and short, stout legs; his ears small, and half-pricked; his head is rather large in proportion to the size of his body, and the muzzle considerably pointed; his scent is extremely acute, so that he can trace the footsteps of all other animals with certainty; he is generally of a sandy color or black. Dogs of these colors are certainly the most hardy, and more to be depended upon; when white or pied, it is a sure mark of the impurity of the breed. The hair of the terrier is long, matted, and hard, over almost every part of his body. His bite is extremely keen. There are three distinct varieties of the Scotch terrier: The one above described. Another, about the size and form, but with hair much longer, and somewhat flowing, which gives his legs the appearance of being very short. This is the prevailing breed of the Western Islands of Scotland. The third variety is much larger than the other two, being generally from fifteen to eighteen inches in height with the hair very hard and wiry, and much shorter than that of the others.

The description of the Scotch Terrier offered a useful delineation with the first mentioned variety apparently the forerunner of what we now know as the Cairn, West Highland White, Dandie Dinmont and Scottish Terrier. The second variety unquestionably defined the Skye and the third variety, now extinct, was probably the progenitor of the Irish Terrier and was also a useful cross with fighting dogs of the Bull Terrier strain.

Two highland terriers rabbiting are the subjects of this painting by P. Jones (1858). Colors varied in the mid-19th Century and ear cropping was not uncommon. *Courtesy of Gerald Massey.*

An early West Highland and a Scottish Terrier, showing long heads. Note the ear pigmentation on the Westie.

Dandie Dinmont by Sir William Allan, R.A. Engraved by Sly. From Waverly Novels, Abbotsford Ed., published 1842.

This description was copied by a host of later authors, generally without credit, and was modified in terms by many others, often to its detriment. Thus, the term Scotch Terrier found in books after 1829 did not necessarily indicate the dog we now know as the Scottish Terrier but was generic to at least three other varieties, to wit, the West Highland White, the Cairn and the Dandie Dinmont. This variation was narrowed down rather quickly to two other breeds since the Dandie gained early independence, probably at a date even before the publication of Brown's book.

The indiscriminate use of the term Scotch Terrier as a designation for Cairns, West Highlands and Scottish Terriers continued for many years. The Scottish Terrier was the first to gain autonomy through club and show activity, followed by the Westie and finally the Cairn, which still bears the closest resemblance to the early Scotch Terrier. In spite of the emergence of separate breeds from the basic blood, there was much interbreeding of these strains even into the 20th century.

The late Walter Reeves, a great Terrier man and all-breed judge, told me that in England and Scotland, around the turn of the century, all three breeds often came from a single litter according to what the buyer wanted. It is also a known fact that West Highland Whites were often classed and shown as Scottish Terriers and were in great demand because of their distinctive color. Cairns, too, fell in this category and records will show that registered dogs of all three breeds often could be found in a single pedigree. Actually, Westies and Cairns were not fully separated until about 1917 through a Kennel Club decree which prohibited interbreeding.

Thus, claims of first birth by proponents of any of these breeds of Scotch descent are ill-founded since students have difficulty in tracing pure blood in any of them before about 1875–1880. The distinct characteristics of Scottish, Cairn and West Highland White Terriers as we know them today are, however, quite different. The conformation of the Scottish Terrier, as will be shown, has been changed the most through the years while the Westie may possibly be a larger dog than his progenitors. The Cairn is gradually being shortened in back but most nearly resembles the early Scotch Terrier, although the ears are now always upright.

27

Teaser, an early winner.

Scotch Terriers at work. By James Robertson, 1835.

The first real move towards breed autonomy by the Scottish Terrier branch from the more generic Scotch Terrier family came about through dog shows, which began in 1859. At this time, those interested in exhibiting their dogs began to realize the need for greater uniformity of type. Then as now, the requirements for a dog to win were determined by the judges who placed the dogs at the shows according to their opinion of what a good 'un should be.

The first recorded, organized dog show was held in England in Newcastle-on-Tyne, June 28th and 29th, 1859 with sixty entries limited to Pointers and Setters. In the following year a show in Birmingham was the first to offer classes for all breeds. Truly, this was a milestone in the development of the purebred family.

The Scotch Terrier made his first appearance in the show ring at Birmingham in 1860, the second year of organized dog shows. Here there was a classification for "Scotch Terriers." The winner of the class was a "White Skye" which adds to the early confusion brought about by the generic breed name. As time went on, dog shows increased the problem of separating the breeds or strains. The classes for Scotch Terriers disappeared and classes for such breeds as Rough-haired Terriers, Aberdeen, Paisley, and Highland Terriers were provided, and dogs of several breeds were entered indiscriminately. According to Gray, Paisley Terriers were silkies and the Rough-haired Terriers were a nondescript lot. To compound the problem, many Scotsmen preferred to call all of their dogs Skyes and frequently exhibited Scottish Terriers types in the Skye Terrier classes. Mr. Gordon Murray was one of these, and when he entered his "Otter," which according to advice was a proper Scottish Terrier, as a Skye at Swindon in 1976, the judges were bitterly denounced for not recognizing it as "a genuine Skye." Thus, the Scottish Terrier had many an alias which caused difficult times. In 1879 the Kennel Club revived separate classes for Scotch Terriers which were quickly assailed by fanciers of the Aberdeen strain who wanted additional classes for their breed. The effort failed, and by 1881 the several varieties were engulfed by the more popular Scotch Terrier classification. About the same time, proponents of the "pure," "genuine," and "hard-coated" Skye became reconciled to call their dogs Hard-haired Scotch Terriers and the turmoil gradually subsided.

This stormy period certainly retarded growth and widespread

29

recognition of the breed and the "Scot's" determination to "make a point" did not hasten the solution of the matter. However, during 1882 some positive moves were made. Vero Shaw wrote a standard for "Hard-Haired Scotch Terriers which was carried in *the Field* on March 28, 1882 and on page 79 of the October 1883 issue of American Kennel Register. After the standard was written a club was formed and was called The Scotch Terrier Club. Rules and regulations were established together with a "Standard of Points" for the Hard-Haired Scotch Terrier which reads as follows:

Points of the Hard-Haired Scotch Terriers

Skull — (Value 5) proportionately long, slightly domed, and covered with short, hard hair about ¾ in. long, or less. It should not be quite flat, as there should be a sort of stop, or drop, between the eyes.

Muzzle — (5) very powerful, and gradually tapering toward the nose, which should always be black and of good size. The jaws should be perfectly level, and the teeth square, though the nose projects somewhat over the mouth, which gives the impression of the upper jaw being longer than the under one.

Eyes — (5) set wide apart, of a dark brown or hazel color; small, piercing, very bright, and rather sunken.

Ears — (10) very small, prick or half-prick (the former is preferable), but never drop. They should also be sharp-pointed, and the hair on them should not be long, but velvety, and they should not be cut. The ears should be free from any fringe at the top.

Neck — (5) short, thick and muscular; strongly set over sloping shoulders.

Chest — (5) broad in comparison to the size of the dog, and proportionately deep.

Body — (10) of moderate length, not so long as a Skye's, and rather flat-sided; but well ribbed up and exceedingly strong in hindquarters.

Legs and Feet — (10) both fore and hindlegs should be short, and very heavy in bone, the former being straight, or slightly bent, and well set on under the body, as the Scotch terrier should not be out at elbows.

The hocks should be bent, and the thighs very muscular; and the feet strong, small, and thickly covered with short hair, the forefeet being larger than the hind ones, and well let down on the ground.

The Tail — (2½), which is never cut, should be about 7 in. long, carried with a slight bend, and often gaily.

The Coat — (2½) steel or iron gray, brindle, black, red, wheaten, and even yellow or mustard color. It may be observed that mustard, black, and red are not usually so popular as the other colors. White markings are most objectionable.

General Appearance — (10) the face should wear a very sharp, bright and active expression, and the head should be carried up. The dog (owing to the shortness of his coat) should appear to be higher on the leg than he really is; but at the same time, he should look compact, and possessed of great muscle in his hindquarters. In fact, a Scotch terrier, though essentially a terrier, cannot be too powerfully put together. He should be from about 9 in. to 12 in. in height, and should have the appearance of being higher on the hind legs than on the fore.

Faults

Muzzle either under or over-hung.

Eyes large or light-colored.

Ears large, round at the points, or drop. It is also a fault if they are too heavily covered with hair.

Coat. Any silkiness, wave, or tendency to curl is a serious blemish, as is also an open coat.

Size. Specimens over 18 lb. should not be encouraged.

Having read the above standard, and considered the same, I am prepared to express my approval of it, and will give it my support when breeding or judging hard-haired Scotch Terriers.

David Adams, Murrygate, Dundee.

J.A. Adamson, Ashley Road, Aberdeen.

Alex Barclay, Springbank Terrace, Aberdeen.

H. Blomfield, Lakenham, Norfolk.

James Burr, M.D., Aberdeen.

J.C. Carrick, Carlisle.

John Cumming, Bridge of Don, Aberdeen.

W.D. Findlay, Portlethen, Aberdeenshire.

Wm. Frazer, Jasmine Terrace, Aberdeen.

John L. Grainger, Summer Street, Aberdeen.

D.J. Thomson Gray, South George Street, Dundee

Pat Henderson, Tally Street, Dundee.

Mary Laing, Granton Lodge, Aberdeen.

P.R. Latham, Tween Terrace, Bridge of Allan.

H.J. Ludlow, St. Giles Plain, Norwich.

Gray's book elaborates upon the standard and offers some additional important comments. For example, "An all-white colour is much prized; but white markings which often appear on the forefeet and chest, are very objectionable." This is another indication that dogs of the West Highland strain were present and acceptable as Scottish Terriers in the ring. However, the early fanciers most valued the "sandy" color for it has been said that "no other word is so expressive of colour, and will readily be understood by all Scotsmen." In spite of all the "points of beauty" insisted upon by fanciers, the working man ignored them if the dog could work, if not, he was a "guid-for-naething useless brute."

31

In spite of the apparent agreement by a number of prominent fanciers who approved the wording of the standard as set forth herein, the club did not flourish. In fact, no stable organization came into being in support of the breed until about 1887 when the Scottish Terrier Club (of England) was formed followed in 1888 by a similar club in Scotland. The problems that beset the several clubs form an interesting chapter in Dr. Ewing's book on the breed which was written by George Davidson, one of the founders of the Scottish club. Some interesting material concerning the 1882 club may be found in Gordon Stable's book, *Our Friend the Dog*, circa 1883, p. 318 et seq.

Of considerable interest to students of the breed's development is the description of a Scotch Terrier offered by Hugh Dalziel of Kirkcudbrigdeshire and author of *British Dogs*. He gave it from memory and referred to dogs known to him in his childhood, about 1840. He described the "true" Scotch Terrier as follows:

> A stoutly built dog, leggy in comparison with the Skye, or Dandie, varying in size, as all breeds little cared for do, but easily to be kept near to a standard of 15 pounds to 18 pounds, which I hold to be the most useful for a working "varmint" dog, even if he is not wanted to go to ground.
>
> The head rather short and the skull somewhat round, the jaws being strong and also short — more or less bearded; long, lean punishing jaw, as the phrase goes, is a modern feature in terriers of any variety, and the idea is often carried to great excess. The eyes bright and keen, piercing through short, shaggy hair. The ears small, covered with soft, short hair, semi-erect, falling over at the tip. The neck short and strong.
>
> The chest moderately deep, ribs strong, the back ones fairly developed; the back short as a fox-terrier's with strong loins and good muscular square buttocks. The legs stout, well covered with hard hair, stifles only moderately bent; forelegs straight, all covered with hard hair; the feet compact and hard in the sole and the claws strong. The tail, if undocked, 8 in. to 10 in. long, brushlike, not fringed, the covering being hard hair. The prevailing colour sandy, sometimes a dark grizzle, and I have occasionally seen them brindled. The coat hard and very dense, from one inch or rather less than two inches in length at the greatest.

Dalziel's description is of utmost interest when compared to the first accepted standard of the Scottish Terrier. The head differs since it appears that Dalziel describes the head of a Cairn or West Highland more accurately than that of a Scottish Terrier. The tail is relatively long and sometimes docked while the standard emphasized "never cut." The most interesting comment in Dalziel's description, however, is the suggestion, "the back short as a fox-ter-

AMERICAN
Kennel Register

Copyright, 1884. Entered at the Post Office as Second Class Matter.

PUBLISHED BY THE FOREST AND STREAM PUBLISHING CO., 39 & 40 PARK ROW.

| P. O. Box 2832. | New York, August, 1884. | VOL. II—No. 8. |

· SCOTCH TERRIERS.
Miss Mary Laing's "Foxie" and Mr. J. A. Adamson's "Roger Rough."

American Kennel Register title page, August 1884.

rier's." The standard suggests that the body be of "moderate length." Both specifications note the ears to be small and while Dalziel's requires a semi-erect ear, the standard prefers a prick ear.

Since the breed had never really become autonomous until after the standard was adopted, it is understandable that few dogs of merit were recorded before that time. Several, however, did gain mention and these were complimented by Shaw in his article that included the standard. Woodcuts of Miss Laing's Foxie by Shârp ex Fan, and Mr. Adamson's Roger Rough by Fury ex Flo, were used and these were later the subject of the frontispiece of the August 1884 issue of the *American Kennel Register*, reproduced here. Shaw's article also gives credit to Messrs. Blomfield and Ludlow's, Bonaccord and Splinter II, both good dogs of the day.

Passing to Gray's *The Dogs of Scotland*, published in 1887 (first book on the breed), we find that Ch. Dundee was considered by the author as the best to that time. He was owned by the Gourock Kennels of Messrs. Mackie and McColl of Glasgow. Dundee, the biggest winner of his day, ruled the shows in Scotland and England from about 1884 through 1886. Dundee carried a stud book number of 16,818 and according to Mr. McColl, one of his breeders, was by Dunotter out of Glenorchy, Dunotter being by Bodach out of Callack and Glenorchy by Dunolly ex Calliach (See Gray's *The Dogs of Scotland*, 1887). Dunolly was also considered a very good specimen at the time.

The interesting point of this pedigree set forth in 1887 is the disparity between it and the lineage offered by Mrs. Dorothy Caspersz in her book, *Scottish Terrier Pedigrees*, compiled in 1934. Mrs. Caspersz, who was one of the greatest modern authorities on Scottish Terriers pedigrees, used an entirely different background. According to this later authority, Ch. Dundee was whelped December 30, 1882; bred by Captain Mackie and by Rambler out of Worry, he did not finish his championship until about 1888. Since Gray's book was published in 1887 and perforce had to be prepared before that, it is evident that Dundee finished before 1887. The major deviation however is found in the breeding, where entirely different parents are given. Mrs. Caspersz undoubtedly followed the same authority as C.J. Davies who in his book *The Scottish Terrier* (1906) said "the statement made in *Dogs of Scotland* (1891 ed.) that the bitch,

THE

DOGS OF SCOTLAND:

THEIR VARIETIES, HISTORY, BREEDING, EXHIBITION, AND MANAGEMENT.

ILLUSTRATED.

By D. J. THOMSON GRAY ("WHINSTONE").

Editor of "The Scottish Fancier and Rural Gazette."

DUNDEE: JAMES P. MATHEW & CO., 17 AND 19 COWGATE.

LONDON: L. UPCOTT GILL, "THE BAZAAR" OFFICE, STRAND, W.C.

EDINBURGH AND GLASGOW: JOHN MENZIES & CO.

1887.

Cover of the book, *Dogs of Scotland*, 1887.

35

Glenorchy became the dam of Ch. Dundee is incorrect." Why it is incorrect he does not say. In any event, the "error" was carried forward in Gray's book from the 1887 edition into the 1891 edition without apparent comment from the many readers. Whatever the answer, this situation points to the many stumbling blocks and pitfalls that confront later authors who wish to present accurate findings. Suffice it to say that Dundee was the third Scottish Terrier to gain the title, according to Mrs. Caspersz, having been preceded by Syringa and the aforementioned Dunolly, bitch and dog, respectively. Mr. McColl writes interestingly of "Old Syringa," which he says like the water and had been seen to stand "in a burn for hours, her head and neck only being above water, watching a rat hole in the embankment."

Some interesting measurements of the two dogs Dunolly and Dundee together with those of a bitch Glengogo, all of the 1880's, are found in *Dogs of Scotland*:

	Dunolly	Dundee	Glengogo
Occipital bone to eye	4⅞ inches	5 inches	4½ inches
Inner corner of eye to nose	3 "	3 "	3 "
Shoulder to root of tail	15 "	15 "	16 "
Length of tail	—	7 "	7½ "
Round muzzle	6⅞ "	7¼ "	6½ "
" skull	11½ "	11¾ "	11½ "
" chest	17¾ "	17½ "	17½ "
" loin	14¾ "	15 "	15 "
" arm	4⅞ "	5 "	4½ "
Height	10 "	10 "	10 "

These measurements indicate that the old Scots were considerably longer in back than present day breed representatives. Surprisingly enough, however, the head measurements indicate substantial length, about seven and one-half to eight inches, while the skull was rather broad in comparison to the muzzle; which should have given the dogs a rather snipy outlook on the Cairn order. Since these dogs weighed from 16 to 18 pounds and had about the same height at the withers as today's specimens it is apparent that the bodies were shallower and the dogs more up on the leg in order to maintain the weight-height proportions. Also the bodies were not as full, and had more of a flattish side appearance of the type now seen on Westies and Cairns.

This was the hectic history of the breed during the long and harried quest for recognition. Known and shown under many names, the breed finally reached its goal with the designation Scottish Terrier which still is accepted, used and respected by all.

> He was a gash an' faithfu' tyke
>
> As ever lap a sheugh or dyke.
>
> His honest sonsie, baws'nt face
>
> Ay gat him friends in ilka place.
>
> ROBERT BURNS

Skittles, an early Scottish Terrier of about 1882.

Ch. Dundee, the third recorded British titleholder.

Ch. Alister won prizes both as a drop-eared and prick-eared exhibit.

4

Scottish Terrier
Bloodlines

ALL Scottish Terriers descended from common blood, but through the years certain dogs have exerted more than their share of influence on the breed. This is indicated by repeated notice of a given sire or sires in the pedigrees of quality dogs.

Because of the excellent pedigree delineations published by Mrs. Dorothy Caspersz (British) and Dr. Kirk (American), together with numerous articles by Alice Exworthy on the bloodlines of the breed, there is little use of going into an exhaustive exposition of the subject here. Those who have a genuine interest may trace families and pedigrees in great detail by referring to these expansive efforts.

Basically, there are two lines of descent which are accountable for the great majority of all Scottish Terriers champions. The first is the Ch. Dundee line, the second the Ch. Alister line. The Dundee line is of disputed origin as noted in the preceding chapter. It may have begun with the dog, Bright, as Mrs. Caspersz suggests, or it may have come from a different origin in accordance with the early book, *The*

Ch. Ems Chevalier, whelped 1904.

Ch. Heworth Rascal, painted by John
Emms, 1902.

Ch. Bonaccord Peggy.

Dogs of Scotland. In either case, starting with Ch. Dundee, the blood passes down through such dogs as Seafield Rascal, Laindon Lockhart, Ch. Albourne Beetle, etc. Thereafter the influence weakens and today the line is of minor importance when compared to the Alister branch of the family tree. This, beyond dispute, came from the aforementioned Bright through Bonaccord to Rambler which begot Ch. Alisa II, Ch. Glengogo and possibly Ch. Dundee. Rambler's best known son was Ch. Alister which came from the bitch Ch. Lorna Doone sired by the aforementioned Dundee.

Alister sired many great dogs in the early days of the breed's development including the first American champion, Tiree; Ch. Kildee, Ch. Mirza, etc. However, the most illustrious of his sons was a dog named Whinstone, probably after the breed authority D.J. Thomson Gray who wrote under the pen-name "Whinstone." This dog's direct male line was propagated through Heather Prince to Claymore, sire of Ch. Claymore Defender. He in turn sired Ch. Seafield Blossom, winner of 26 Challenge Certificates, thus tying the record previously held by Ch. Bonnaccord Nora; Ch. Tighnavarloch, J. Dean Willis' great and productive stud Ch. Bapton Norman (a black with an extremely short body for the day) which sired six English and ten American champions and also had the distinction in 1912 of siring more litters in the United States than any other American or British stud; and last but by no means least, Bapton Noble, a brother to Norman, whose great grandson, Ch. Laindon Luminary, became a key dog in the Alister line.

Luminary produced a number of champion get but it was his son Albourne Joe that carried on through a son, Ch. Albourne Adair. This dog was prolific as a stud but two of his get will always be remembered because they were the fountainheads of bloodlines that are of greatest importance today. These two dogs were Ch. Albourne Scot and Ch. Albourne MacAdair. The first produced Ch. Albourne Barty through a union with Albourne Jennifer. Barty became one of the great dogs of the breed; he was whelped on September 17, 1925 and his breeder was the master of Albourne Kennels, Mr. A.G. Cowley. More will be offered about this great dog and his influence upon present day bloodlines later.

The second, Ch. Albourne MacAdair, sired a dog named Harton Highlander which in turn produced the incomparable Ch. Heather

Necessity (whelped on September 14, 1927). The facts leading up to this event are of considerable interest since they demonstrate that all great dogs do not necessarily come from carefully planned breedings. It seems that a Mr. Herbert Bains, known as a breeder of several Terrier breeds, bought a bitch named Harton Holdfast. She was said to have been a good one, well bred but no flyer. He showed her nonetheless at Manchester with indifferent success. While at the show he discussed her future with William McCandlish, the famous judge and a good breeder, who advised that she be mated. Since she was in season at the time and since Ch. Albourne MacAdair had won the breed on the day and was available, the mating was arranged on the spot. The litter produced five puppies including one dog. He was named Harton Highlander and was later sold to Sam Wilson, a breeder and judge who held the dog at stud. Highlander was later bred to a biggish bitch of good quality named Skerne Scotch Lass and the result was Necessity, originally named "Snooker's Double."

Robert Chapman ultimately acquired the dog that turned out to be one of the all-time greats, a 20-certificate winner and the sire of some 18 English and 12 American champions together with a host of other fine Scottish Terriers. Chapman, after buying Necessity, demonstrated a breeder's instinct and purchased Skerne Scotch Lass. She too proved to be an excellent investment as will be seen.

It is interesting to observe that many of Necessity's best offspring came from bitches closely line-bred to Ch. Albourne Barty. This is understandable upon study of Necessity's pedigree, which defies all the precepts of good breeding practice and presents a host of unrelated ancestors in a pedigree devoid of any semblance of line breeding. In spite of his background, Necessity had something that few dogs own, that illusive quality, "prepotency." Many will say that there is no such thing. On the other hand, Necessity was bred to many bitches that, according to principle, should not nick because of background, but these same bitches produced offspring that made history.

Take for example, Ch. Lonkley Larkspur, Ch. Heather Enchantress, Ch. Heather Fashion Hint and Ch. Ortley Elegance, to name a few; all were by Necessity but in no case can a common ancestor be found within the first five generations of their pedigrees, which

The great Ch. Heather Necessity.

			Albourne Joe
		Eng. Ch. Albourne Adair	
			Eng. Ch. Albourne Dinkie
	Eng. Ch. Albourne MacAdair		
			Ruminantly Rocket
		Albourne Matron	
Harton Highlander			
			Biddick Boy
		Loyal Boy	
			Loyal Ann
	Harton Holdfast		
			Claymore Conqueror
		Glenbrae Betty	
			Monnyruy
ENG. CH. HEATHER NECESSITY			
(Whelped 9/14/1927			Romany Monk
Breeder: Mr. Walker)		Ornsay Chieftain	
			Tantallon Vixen
	Eng. Ch. Ornsay Brave		
			Misty Morning
		Eng. Ch. Bellstane Lassie	
			Meadow Lass
Skerne Scotch Lass			
			Romany Bishop
		Abertay Aristocrat	
			Abertay Darkie
	Meg		
			Abertay Brigadier
		Fanny	
			Tattle

certainly is contrary to all accepted principles of line breeding. The fact remains, Necessity had so much quality, so much to give, that he carried over in spite of the bloodlines. No one can ever say that this dog lacked prepotency because the record proves the statement false.

In addition to the above noted offspring, Ch. Heather Necessity was responsible for such dogs as Ch. Rookery Adair, Ch. Heather Essential of Hitofa, Ch. Sandhey's Silvertip, Ch. Rouken Rogue, Ch. Heather Ambition, Ch. Albourne Royalist and Ch. Crich Certainty of Deephaven. Certainly these names are widely known today as each did his share to bring the breed to its present position. Ch. Heather Essential of Hitofa, exported to the United States, sired among others Ch. Hillcote Laddie which in turn sired some 15 title-holders including Ch. Deephaven Warspite, a great show dog that led the breed in the United States in 1945 and 1946.

Ch. Heather Ambition did his part to maintain the family's blood by siring among others Ch. Ortley Pilot, Ch. Heather Beau Ideal, Ch. Heather Independence (whose great-grandson, Ch. Shieling's Signature, sired 22 champions and in addition won the Garden in 1945) and Bradthorn Banker, sire of the great Ch. Bradthorn Bullion, one of the stalwarts of the once famous Relgalf Kennels.

Ch. Heather Fashion Hint, Necessity's most prolific son, sired 14 English and 26 American titleholders. These included Ch. Radical of Rookes, Eng. Ch. Masterpiece of Rookes, Ch. Dandy of Docken, Ch. Walsing Wallet, and Eng. Ch. Heather Realisation, which proved to be a prepotent stud with such get as Ch. Walsing Warrant of Marlu, the grandsire of Ch. Deephaven Red Seal (sire of 24 U.S. Chs. including Ch. Goldfinder's Admiral and Ch. Marlu Clincher), Heather Benefactor and Heather Herald. This last named dog produced Kennelgarth Blacksmith; he was responsible for Reanda Roderic, the sire of Eng. Ch. Reanda Roger Rough that produced many good ones including the Barberry Knowe Kennel's Ch. Walsing Wild Winter.

Heather Benefactor, by Realisation, sired Walsing Wizard which in turn fathered two great sons, Walsing Watchtower and Westpark Masterpiece. The first of these is behind such widely known winners as Ch. Walsing Lomond Lancer of Hampton Hill, Ch. Glendoune Gauntlet, Ch. Reanda Rheola, Ch. Bardene Boy Blue, Ch. Wyre-

Ch. Heather Essential of Hitofa, owned by Hill-Top Farm Kennels.

Heather Benefactor, noted winner and sire of the 1930s with the BIS trophy he won at Edinburgh in 1938.

Ch. Heather Fashion Hint.

			Eng. Ch. Albourne Adair
		Eng. Ch. Albourne MacAdair	
	Harton Highlander		Albourne Matron
			Loyal Boy
		Harton Holdfast	
Eng. Ch. Heather Necessity			Glenbrae Betty
			Ornsay Chieftain
		Eng. Ch. Ornsay Brave	
	Skerne Scotch Lass		Eng. Ch. Bellstane Lassie
			Abertay Aristocrat
		Meg	
			Fanny

ENG. CH. HEATHER FASHION HINT
(Whelped 6/2/1929
Breeder: J. Donald)

			Eng. Ch. Laurieston Leaper
		Eng. Ch. Laurieston Landseer	
	Laurieston Ladeside		Garnqueen Gertrude
			Garnock Bertie
		Carmel Kate	
Innerkip Irma			Carmel Betty
			Ornsay Ranger
		Garnock Bob	
	Innerkip Nanette		Garnock Jean
			Ornsay Bannock
		Garnock Ura	
			Garnock Kate

bury Woodnymph and Ch. Glendoune Gaytime (dam of five champions), to name a few. Masterpiece was even more prolific, with Eng. Chs. Roskeen Banner, Westpark Masterman, Westpark Achievement, Am. Ch. Trevone Tartar of Bothkennar, a great sire in America, and the redoubtable Eng. Ch. Westpark Rio Grande. The last named sired 21 American titleholders in addition to Eng. Ch. Westpark Romeo, father of the great Ch. Westpark Derriford Baffie which proved to be an outstanding producer both in England and the United States. Another great and prolific son of Westpark Rio Grande, the dog Ch. Wyrebury Wrangler, produced three great bitches in Chs. Wyrebury Water Gypsy, dam of five champions, Niddbank Ladybird, Walsing Winoway and the dogs, Ch. Crescent Hill Ace O'Spades and Ch. Wyrebury Wilwyn. The latter fathered Ch. Special Edition, sire of Ch. Scotvale Sunshine and Ch. Wycheworth Wizard, among others.

To enlarge further upon the progeny and family of Ch. Heather Necessity would amount to dedicating this book to his achievements, since the list is never ending. Many great dogs have not been mentioned and many tie-ins with present day winners have not been noted. Suffice it to say, Ch. Heather Necessity was one of the greatest of Scottish Terrier sires and his efforts undoubtedly were responsible for a major part of the success of the breed as we know it today. In fact few pedigrees can be extended without noting Necessity in the background. Possibly this may be explained by discussing the dog briefly.

Necessity has been described as a "new" type Scotsman for the day. He represented a transition between the old and the new types. It has been said that never before had a Scottish Terrier had such length of head, compactness of body and straightness of leg. He was lower to the ground than his forebears, owned a short back and a short, inverted carrot-shaped tail that was always carried stiffly erect, even when the dog was sitting. Some said that he could never do the work for which the breed was intended and many decried the radical change in type that this jet black dog presented. Nevertheless most of his critics bred their bitches to him in hope of obtaining something that would look, produce and win as he did. From his list of accomplishments it is easy to say that many of these breeders were not disappointed in the results. Necessity was surely one of the greatest studs the breed has ever known.

Returning to Ch. Albourne Barty, we find that while he was not as prolific as Necessity he nevertheless sired some great dogs and a host of important bitches that helped establish quality and wide breed recognition. In fact the Barty line is equally as important as that of Necessity. He sired among others the brothers Ch. Albourne Brigand, in whose line we find Ch. Blanart Barrister, sire of some 14 U.S. Champions, and Ch. Albourne Reveller, both out of that great brood bitch Albourne Annie Laurie. Reveller gained fame by producing Ch. Heather Reveller of Sporran, a great winner in this country and a dog that gained an excellent press because of his record and the prominence of his owner, the late S.S. Van Dine. Surveying Heather Reveller's pedigree we see that the dog was out of Skerne Scotch Lass, which was also the dam of Ch. Heather Necessity. Here we find that Chapman's foresight in quickly buying the bitch after he acquired Necessity was a very smart and useful move. In Reveller the two branches of the Albourne Adair blood were reunited and the effort proved to be quite productive for he was not only a great show dog but a good sire. Albourne Binge Result, another son of Albourne Reveller, was responsible for one of the all-time show greats in Eng. Ch. Albourne Admiration. This dog was a 20-certificate winner and the only Scottie to tie Necessity's record to that time. He was the result of a half-brother–half-sister breeding since his dam, Elspeth Judy, was also sired by Reveller. Thus the blood behind Admiration had a heavy Barty influence blended through both sides of his genealogy. Admiration founded a line that extended through his grandson, Ch. Malgren Juggernaut to Ch. Walsing Winning Trick of Edgerstoune. Winning Trick was the top winning Scottie in America during 1949 and was the winner of the Garden in 1950. He sired 23 titleholders in this country including Ch. Edgerstoune Troubadour, sire of 35 champions, one of the greatest of modern-day studs. Troubadour's name appears in the pedigrees of such dogs as Ch. Rebel Raider, Ch. Fulluvit Festive Fling, Ch. Rebel Invader and Ch. Fulluvit Fieldmouse, among others. In addition to his siring ability, the dog won some of tⁱ ᵕ largest shows in the country during his long and fruitful ring career, a worthy son of the great Winning Trick.

Ch. Edgerstoune Troubadour, painted by C.C. Fawcett.

			Albourne Samson
		Malgen Juggernaut	
			Malgen Jerusha
	Walsing War Parade		
			Walsing Winebibber
		Walsing Wishing	
			Walsing Wishbone
Ch. Walsing Winning Trick of Edgerstoune			
			Walsing Wizard
		Walsing Watchmaker	
			Glencannie Sonia
	Walsing Whymper		
			Hillhead Ambassador
		Walsing Wildwind	
			Kilette

CH. EDGERSTOUNE TROUBADOUR
(Whelped 7/13/1949
Breeder: Mrs. J.G. Winant)

			Ch. Ortley Ambassador of E.
		Ch. Heather Resolution of E.	
			Desco Dream
	Ch. Heather Commodore of Edgerstoune		
			Walsing Winebibber
		Walsing Wishing	
			Walsing Wishbone
Ch. Edgerstoune Orphan			
			Ortley Matador
		Ch. Ortley Ambassador of E.	
			Ortley Bibby
	Edgerstoune Ophelia		
			Heather Beau Ideal
		Ch. Heather Ophelia of E.	
			Gaisgill Vanity

The famous Ch. Albourne Scot, sire of Ch. Albourne Barty.

Ch. Albourne Admiration.

There are several other dogs of more recent vintage that merit acclaim as productive sires. The first of these is surely Ch. Bardene Bingo, a great show dog, best in show winner at Westminster (1967) and a prepotent sire with some 45 titleholders to his credit. More recently, Ch. Gaidoune Great Bear eclipsed all records to his time by siring 53 champions through 1974. That records are only made to be broken was evidenced four years later when Ch. Anstamm Happy Venture reached a mark of 59 titleholders, making him the all-time top producer to then. He died in 1979. One other dog, owned by the Stamms, was also a fine producer. This was Ch. Bardene Boy Blue, who sired forty champions. Of course, there are many other fine studs, the dogs mentioned have been fortunate in having been bred to a number of quality bitches owned in many instances by breeders who knew how to raise young stock for the best results possible. Further, because of the show overtones involved with all the dogs mentioned, many of their offspring were sought for show purposes which surely enhanced their sires' opportunitites even further. What must be remembered is that many worthy stud dogs never had the opportunity to breed a representative number of high-quality bitches. This fact surely limited their influence on the breed. There is no better formula toward success than to work with dogs from high quality parents — it is an acknowledged fact.

While the foregoing has been limited in a large degree to the accomplishments of selected stud dogs, several outstanding bitches of the past have also been mentioned. Admittedly, there are many, many more, but because of the limited number of offspring that any one bitch is capable of producing, the importance of the distaff side of the pedigree is difficult to document with proper credit to the many that have contributed to the success of the breed. For these reasons, no extensive digression into the female's part in the breed's development will be offered. However, two bitches from the present day stand out so completely that they bear mention among the all-time greats since each one has productively outdistanced all of their forebears. These are Ch. Blanart Barcarolle and Ch. Gaidoune Gorgeous Hussy.

Barcarolle's pedigree offers an interesting blend of producing blood. Her sire, Cabrach Caliper, goes back through the tail male

51

Ch. Blanart Barcarolle.

			Cabrach Reek
		Ch. Cabrach Calibar	
	Diehard Fashion		Cabrach Cheetah
			Heather Romancer
		Diehard Viola II	
Cabrach Caliper			Diehard Viola
			Ch. Cabrach Tanner
		Cabrach Poker	
	Cabrach Dot		Cabrach Classic
			Ch. Cabrach Calibar
		Cabrach Glamor	
			Tower Hill Glamor

CH. BLANART BARCAROLLE
(Whelped 6/20/1947
Breeder: Blanche E. Reeg)

			Eng. Ch. Heather Fashion Hint
		Eng. Ch. Heather Realisation	
	Flornell Real Fashion		Gaisgill Sylvia
			Eng. Ch. Heather Fashion Hint
		Bradthorn Black Berry	
Hi-Scott's Clipper			Arns Ruby
			Ch. Bradthorn Bullion
		Blanart Bomber	
	Black Eyed Susan IX		Hi-Scott's Penny Wise
			Dalreoch Resounder
		Franfield's Sweet Heather	
			Franfield's Merrymaker

Ch. Gaidoune Gorgeous Hussy.

                                    Walsing War Parade
                        Ch. Walsing Winning Trick of Edgerstoune
                                    Walsing Whymper
            Ch. Edgerstoune Troubadour
                                    Ch. Heather Commodore of E.
                        Ch. Edgerstoune Orphan
                                    Edgerstoune Ophelia
    Ch. Rebel Raider
                                    Walsing War Parade
                        Ch. Walsing Winning Trick of Edgerstoune
                                    Walsing Whymper
            Marlu Cute Trick
                                    Ch. Deephaven Warspite
                        Ch. Marlu Sassy Lassie
                                    Marlu Miss Heather

CH. GAIDOUNE GORGEOUS HUSSY
(Whelped 9/30/1956   Eng. Ch. Wyrebury Wonder
Breeder: Helen Gaither)   Eng. Ch. Wyrebury Welldoer
                                    Wyrebury Dream of Dockindee
            Glendoune Gay Boy
                                    Glendoune Galcador
                        Glendoune Gadabout
                                    Glendoune Gorgeous
    Ch. Glendoune Gaibonnie
                                    Rosehall Enchanter
                        Ch. Rosehall Toryglen Tam O'Shanter
                                    Rosehall Miranda
            Eng. Ch. Glendoune Gipsy
                                    Medwal Midshipman
                        Rosehall.Brocade
                                    Judy of Tapton

line to the aforementioned Ch. Albourne Barty with a double cross of Ch. Heather Necessity included. Her dam, Hi-Scott's Clipper, goes through Ch. Heather Realisation to Necessity; whereby both sides trace back directly to Ch. Albourne Adair. With such a background it is little wonder that this bitch did so well. When bred to Diehard Toby she produced Ch. Blanart Barrister. A glance at Barrister's pedigree will show that Toby represents a double cross of Diehard Fashion blood, the grandsire of Barcarolle. Thus three of the four great grandsires of Barrister are Diehard Fashion, which surely intensifies the line. Ch. Blanart Bewitching, a great show bitch and winner of two Garden Terrier groups, has strong Barcarolle blood, as she was by a son and out of a granddaughter of Barcarolle's. Thus, it is apparent that good breeding tells and intensification of prepotent blood more frequently than not leads to success.

Possibly Barcarolle's best known son was Ch. Blanart Bolero, sire of 20 U.S. titleholders, which was sired by Ch. Barberry Knowe Rascal. Rascal was a good nick with Barcarolle and represented a double cross of Ch. Albourne Barty blood to further intensify this prepotent line. In all Barcarolle produced ten champion offspring.

Ch. Gaidoune Gorgeous Hussy again lends proof that "blood will tell." She is by Ch. Rebel Raider ex Ch. Glendoune Gaibonnie. Raider was by Troubadour bred to his half-sister, Marlu Cute Trick. Thus, Raider offered a double cross of Walsing Winning Trick on the sire's side to team up with Walsing Watchtower blood on the dam's, which intensified the influence of Necessity. This again proves that line breeding is the surest means of producing good stock. Hussy, when bred to Ch. Todhill's Cinnamon Bear, whelped top show dogs on two different occasions. The first was Ch. Gaidoune Great Bear, one of the great show Terriers of his time and the second, Ch. Gaidoune Grin and Bear It, who was also an outstanding show dog. These are but two of her twelve champion offspring from four litters by three different studs. The reason for the success of the Cinnamon Bear breeding is not surprising since he was by Ch. Friendship Farm Diplomat ex Todhill's Beeswing and is line bred to Necessity on both sides.

This short discourse on the accomplishments of two great bitches could be extended to include many more worthy females. In each instance however, it would be found that strong line breeding is and always has been the surest way to produce quality animals. In the chapter on breeding an explanation of the reasons for this statement will be found.

Ch. Friendship Farm Diplomat.

Ch. Gaidoune Great Bear.

"Torphichen Darroch"   "Torphichen Badger"   "Toronto Chief"

This painting, presented to the author by the late Ben Brown, should be of great interest to fanciers as a contrast to the modern Scottish Terrier. The dogs here are (from left) Torphichen Darroch, Torphichen Badger and Toronto Chief.

5

British Breeders and Kennels

In the preceding chapter on early history and blood-lines many famous breeders have been mentioned because of dogs they owned or bred which became landmarks in the progress of the Scottish Terrier. This chapter will enlarge to some extent upon the breeders and kennels in Britain from the beginning of the breed's recognition until the present, and will also attempt to offer some interesting sidelights to supplement previous information.

As designated heretofore, it all began with the early recognition of the breed in the 1800's when such men as Captain Mackie, co-owner with Mr. McColl of the famous Gourock Kennels in Glasgow; John Adamson of Aberdeen, breeder of Ashley Nettle, whose interest was still strong after World War I; D.J. Thomson Gray, and others began to make the Scottish Terrier an individual breed apart from the other varieties of Scotch Terriers known and produced at the time. They were aided by many others, for example, Mr. B. McMillan of Abertay Kennels in Dundee, whose alliance continued for almost 60 years and went back to the days before breed recognition. H.J. Ludlow, breeder of the famous Chs. Aisla II, Lorna Doone, Alister and others; M.L. McDonald, Dunolly's breeder, and William McCandlish; to these and many more we owe a great debt for establishing a new and officially recognized breed.

During the last decade of the 19th century another man came on the scene who, with his sons, left an indelible mark on the history and improvement of the breed. This was Robert Chapman of Glenboig, Scotland. He bred his first champion, Heather Queen, in 1896 and continued until his death, whereupon the Heather Kennels were carried on by his sons, one of the same name, until into the 1930's. Throughout its history, the kennel presented a strong stud force and was a major competitor in the show ring. Prior to World War I, it was not unusual to find 100 or more dogs in its pens. Of course during the conflict, operations were curtailed, as was the case with all other establishments, but when the war ended the younger Chapmans began to rebuild the stud force. From about 1927 to 1935, Heather gained its greatest prominence. Records show that through the years 1930, '31 and '32, dogs owned by Heather together with their progeny dominated the breed and captured 108 out of a possible 132 challenge certificates available to the breed at all recognized shows that offered them.

The Chapmans seldom failed to recognize promise and quality in a young dog. They bought many a likely looking youngster and waited until maturity before deciding whether or not the dog would do. One of their most important purchases was Ch. Albourne Barty from A.G. Cowley in 1927 before the dog had reached his full promise, but he was already a definite comer. In fact, in 1928 Barty was well recognized but overshadowed by his kennel mate, Ch. Merlewood Aristocrat, which held sway during 1928-29.

Chapman's other prize purchase was, of course, Snooker's Double in 1928, which proved to be a stroke of genius. Renamed Heather Necessity, the dog did well from the start but was not immediately included in Chapman's first line, as evidenced by the advertising statement made in late 1929 which read, "Another high class dog is Heather Necessity. He is a good winner and with ordinary luck should have a great future." Chapman did not know how prophetic this statement would become. As mentioned before, Barty bitches bred to Necessity were particularly productive and thus the whole formula was concentrated in one kennel.

58

A classic assembly of the Heather stud before the home at Glenboig.

Ch. Heather Reveller of Sporran.

Ch. Heather Gold Finder.

			Eng. Ch. Albourne MacAdair
		Harton Highlander	
			Harton Holdfast
	Eng. Ch. Heather Necessity		
			Eng. Ch. Ornsay Brave
		Skerne Scotch Lass	
			Meg
Eng. Ch. Heather Fashion Hint			
			Eng. Ch. Laurieston Landseer
		Laurieston Ladeside	
			Carmel Kate
	Innerkip Irma		
			Garnock Bob
		Innerkip Nanette	
			Garnock Ura

ENG. CH. HEATHER REALISATION
(Whelped 1/17/1934
Breeder: R. Chapman)

			Harton Highlander
		Eng. Ch. Heather Necessity	
			Skerne Scotch Lass
	Eng. Ch. Sandheys Silvertip		
			Albourne MacAndy
		Albourne Annie Laurie	
			Eng. Ch. Mischief of Docken
Gaisgill Sylvia			
			Albourne MacAndy
		Marksman of Docken	
			Eng. Ch. Mischief of Docken
	Gaisgill Ling		
			Eng. Ch. Laindon Lancelot
		Crogsland Bess	
			Crogsland Queen

Pedigree of Eng. Ch. Heather Realisation

```
                                              Eng. Ch. Laindon Luminary
                          Albourne Joe
                                              Eng. Ch. Laindon Lightsome
            Eng. Ch. Albourne Adair
                                              Eng. Ch. Albourne Beetle
                          Eng. Ch. Albourne Dinkie
                                              Albourne Young Gyp
  Eng. Ch. Albourne Scot
                                              Eng. Ch. Ruminantly Raven
                          Binnie Boy
                                              Abertay Maud
            Fragments
                                              Baltimore
                          Florida
                                              Albourne Finesse
ENG. CH. ALBOURNE BARTY
(Whelped 9/17/1925                            Abertay Brigadier
Breeder: A.G. Cowley      Eng. Ch. Laindon Luminary
                                              Abertay Luna
            Eng. Ch. Laindon Lumen
                                              Claymore Commandant
                          Eng. Ch. Laindon Lightsome
                                              Abertay Bliss
  Albourne Jennifer
                                              Eng. Ch. Albourne Adair
                          Eng. Ch. Albourne Adonis
                                              Albourne Matron
            Albourne Free Love
                                              Eng. Ch. Albourne Adair
                          Eng. Ch. Albourne Alisa
                                              Albourne Huffy
```

Pedigree of Eng. Ch. Albourne Barty.

```
                                              Eng. Ch. Albourne Adair
                          Eng. Ch. Albourne MacAdair
                                              Albourne Matron
            Harton Highlander
                                              Loyal Boy
                          Harton Holdfast
                                              Glenbrae Betty
  Eng. Ch. Heather Necessity
                                              Ornsay Chieftain
                          Eng. Ch. Ornsay Brave
                                              Eng. Ch. Bellstane Lassie
            Skerne Scotch Lass
                                              Abertay Aristocrat
                          Meg
                                              Fanny
ENG. CH. HEATHER AMBITION
(Whelped 9/30/1931                            Eng. Ch. Albourne Adair
Breeder: Mr. and Mrs. A.M. Robb)  Eng. Ch. Albourne Scot
                                              Fragments
            Eng. Ch. Albourne Barty
                                              Eng. Ch. Laindon Lumen
                          Albourne Jennifer
                                              Albourne Free Love
  Eng. Ch. Albourne Romance
                                              Eng. Ch. Albourne Adair
                          Eng. Ch. Albourne MacAdair
                                              Albourne Matron
            Albourne Athene
                                              Eng. Ch. Albourne Adair
                          Albourne Unity
                                              Albourne Mode
```

Pedigree of Eng. Ch. Heather Ambition.

61

Necessity turned out to be one of the all-time greats in the breed yet many owned him, and not until he was purchased by Chapman was he apparently wanted. Bred by Mr. Walker on September 14, 1927, he was sold to a Mr. Leslie who showed him as a youngster with a catalogue claiming price of 100 pounds. A.G. Cowley quickly picked him up and immediately resold him to Chapman for 200 pounds, a tidy profit. Cowley's name did not even appear in the transaction which, according to Kennel Club records, indicates that Leslie transferred the dog directly to Chapman.

Returning to the Heather Kennels, it is interesting to note the concentration of the stud force at Blenboig during the hieght of its success. In 1928 it included Ch. Merlewood Aristocrat, Ch. Albourne Barty and Heather Necessity, to say nothing of Albourne Brigand and Ornsay Hustler. By 1932 such dogs as Ch. Rich Certainty, Ch. Heather Ambition and the great Ch. Heather Fashion Hint had been added to this already potent group. Little wonder that the kennel was a standout.

The Chapmans' interests were not tied to Scotties alone. In their extensive operation they had many other breeds, which from time to time included Fox Terriers, Alsatians, Gordon Setters and even some Clydesdale horses. In addition, Heather was the starting location for many who have since made their mark in the breed. Chief among these is the Murphy family represented for many years by Tom Murphy, the kennel manager. He in turn employed the brothers Harry, Jimmy and Johnny Murphy, his nephews, as kennel help and it was in this environment that they obtained their training with Scots. The late Robert Gorman also acquired his experience at Heather. He, of course, was later engaged by Mrs. Winant to take over her Edgerstoune Kennels. Thus, Heather Kennels, in addition to being one of the great establishments in Scottish Terriers, was the training ground for many whose efforts did so much to further the breed in this country.

It should be pointed out that the Chapmans would buy anything of quality which they believed would be useful to them. For this reason the breeding record of the kennel, while good, is not startling when compared with its longevity and the size of the establishment. Robert Chapman, Sr. bred some eight titleholders from 1896 to 1906 while his son Robert bred an additional six from 1929 to 1934.

THE "HEATHER" SCOTTISH TERRIERS,

Belonging to
Mr. ROBERT CHAPMAN
Glenboig,
Scotland

CH. HEATHER AMBITION.

CH. HEATHER FASHION HINT
Sire of three Champions.

CH. HEATHER NECESSITY

CH. HEATHER AMBITION
Property of Mr. James Chapman.

CH. ALBOURNE BARTY
Sire of seven Champions.

CH. HEATHER NECESSITY
Winner of twenty Challenge Certificates and Sire of twelve Champions.

HEATHER EXCELLENCE.

CH. CRICH CERTAINTY.

HEATHER SPELLBINDER

CH. U.S.A. ALBOURNE VINDICATED OF BENTLEY.

HEATHER RADIANT.

HEATHER ADELINE.

Heather Kennels' advertisement showing the strength of their stud force.

63

James Chapman, another son, took up the challenge in 1934 and bred seven more, so that by 1944 the Chapman family total of British champions was 21 during a period of 48 years.

This record does not compare with another great name in the breed, that of a contemporary, A.G. Cowley of Horley, Surrey, whose Albourne prefix is still a famous trademark in the breed. Cowley bred Albourne Beetle, his first champion, in 1915. Beetle was subsequently imported into the United States by R.M. Cadwalader's Fairwold Kennels and placed best Scottie at Westminster in 1921. Cowley's record from 1915 through 1934 totalled 23 champions. This was no mean accomplishment when working under the English Kennel Club rules, which limit the number of challenge certificates available. Of course, Cowley's greatest accomplishment was Ch. Albourne Barty, which was sold to Chapman, but many other Albourne dogs were famous both in Britain and America. One of these, Albourne Annie Laurie, rivals Barty in the records as a great one. Annie Laurie is considered by many as the top producing matron of all time, and her record supports this high regard. She was the dam of six champions including Chs. Albourne Brigand, Albourne Reveller and Albourne Braw Lass in a single litter. Ch. Albourne Reveller, considered one of the best Scots ever bred, proved his worth by siring the great Ch. Heather Reveller of Sporran when he was bred to Skerne Scotch Lass, Necessity's dam. Albourne Reveller, like so many of Cowley's dogs, eventually joined the stud force at Heather kennels.

Cowley was probably the most astute breeder in the history of the breed in Britain. He knew the formula for continued success and bred good ones by this formula consistently throughout his long and fruitful career. He offered some of his secrets to the fancy in an article carried by the 1931 Christmas issue of *Our Dogs*, which said:

> To breed champions and to continue to breed champions, one must have a strain and must stick to type by inbreeding. All of the best-known strains of livestock are inbred, and, in fact, we must inbreed to produce a type and to stick to that type. To mate bitches to dogs of different blood is, in 99 cases out of 100, to breed nothing but rubbish. It is because the general run of breeders do these stupid things — often after asking advice which they do not take — that it is left to the very few in each breed to attain success and to keep the high position they hold. [It is believed that the reference to "inbreeding" is directed more correctly to "line breeding" since Cowley was interested basically in breeding within the same bloodlines.]

Mrs. Dorothy Caspersz, long dean of the breed.

A group of famous champions.

This is certainly good advice which, as Cowley says, is asked for but seldom heeded by the average breeder. It is also the reason why some breeders advance and others do not. The concepts behind the success of Cowley's formula will be expanded upon in the chapter on breeding in this book. In any event, the Master of Albourne had the formula; he practiced what he preached and he sold many good ones both in Britain and in the United States for the best interests of the breed and the good name of "Albourne."

Many other names were prominent during the same era which embraced the years until the start of World War II, when breeding operations all but ceased in Britain. The Barlae Kennels of William Prentice at Haddington, Scotland was one of these. Prentice was not only an able breeder but a capable handler as well. His first title-holder was Barlae Proof bred in 1917. He was also widely known for his Cairn and West Highland White Terriers. Prentice later moved his kennels and family to America where the name Prentice became a legend through his accomplishments, followed by those of his son Phil and his daughter Florence, all great Scottish Terrier experts.

The Jhelum Kennels of G.D. Lyell of Brockenhurst, Hampshire, began in the early twenties with the purchase of Ch. Albourne Adonis, which headed a stud force including Littlebury Puck. Puck was a son of Ch. Laindon Luminary, which gained his title in 1920 and was one of a strong kennel owned by Mr. H.R.B. Tweed at Billericay, Essex. Laindon Kennels was active as early as 1906 when Mr. Tweed bred his first champion in Laindon Locket. Through more than 20 years of operations some six champions were bred, which included the aforementioned Luminary, Ch. Laindon Lumen, Ch. Laindon Lightsome and Ch. Laindon Lancelot, among others.

Other kennels of merit were Garnock, owned by Robert Houston of Kilburnie which, active for more than two decades, began operations around the turn of the century; Andrew H. Lister's Rothesay Kennels at Rothesay, Scotland; George Davidson's Merlewood Kennels at Hawick, Scotland, which bred such dandies as Ch. Merlewood Rose, Ch. Merlewood Cleopatra and Ch. Merlewood Hopeful, later exported to the U.S.; the Gaisgill Kennels of Mrs. C.M. Cross

Ch. Sandheys Sheriff, owned by Mrs. F.E. Fowler.

Ch. Ortley Angela.

Eng. and Am. Ch. Merlewood Hopeful.

Ch. Bramble No Less

at Elstree in Hertfordshire, which was a strong establishment that exported many to the States; and the Sandheys Kennels of Mr. Richard Lloyd at Birkdale that once owned the aforementioned Albourne Annie Laurie. Many Sandheys dogs, such as Ch. Sandheys Silvertip, are well known even today.

An establishment that made a quick success story was the Ortley Kennels of Conrad Bremer at Hull, Yorks. Beginning operations about 1930, its rapid rise to the top was due to sound breeding techniques that produced many good ones. Ch. Ortley Carmen, her dam Ch. Ortley Elegance, Ch. Ortley Patience, and Ch. Ortley Ambassador are a few. A number of Ortley dogs came to the U.S. and did well as will be noted later. Quite active into the early fifties Ortley bred about 14 English champions. Sam Bamford, owner of the Walnut Kennels, was widely known in both Britain and the U.S. Dogs bearing the Walnut prefix made their mark in both countries and some 16 Walnut Scotties that came to the kennels of Dr. F.W. Zimmerman at Youngstown, Ohio, made their U.S. titles. Glenisla Kennels, owned by Mr. and Mrs. A.M. Robb of Glenboig, neighbors of Chapman's, owned a well known bitch in Ch. Albourne Romance the dam of such greats as Chs. Heather Essential and Heather Ambition, while the Rookes Kennels of John Sharp of near Halifax owned Ch. Heather Fashion Queen, Grey Steel of Rookes and Ch. Masterpiece of Rookes.

The late W.M. (Max) Singleton was long a highly regarded breeder all around the world and, in the post-war era, dean of the breed in England. He died on April 18, 1976 while serving as president of the Scottish Terrier Club of England, a post that he had held continuously since 1947, an indication of his popularity with breeders of the Scotsman. Singleton bred his first champion, Walsing Whisper by Ch. Heather Necessity, in 1930 and she became the fountainhead for some dozen or more titleholders at the Walsing establishment. Of course, the dog, Ch. Walsing Winning Trick of Edgerstoune was the most famous of all Walsing products. He amassed a fantastic record in America for his owner, Mrs. John G. Winant, topping it off with a best in show at Westminster in 1950. Another good winner exported to the United States was the dog, Ch. Walsing Wild Winter of Barberry Knowe who did so well for the Charles Stalters. Mr. Singleton judged in America several times and proved to be a popular arbiter as well as a charming personality. He judged the national club's 1949 winter specialty in New York and placed, Ch. Independent Ben best of breed.

The War practically stopped dog breeding in England and Scotland. Food was scarce and thoughts of survival came first in most British minds. In spite of this condition, a few staunch breeders kept a bitch or two and shared their scant rations with them. They even enjoyed a few shows during the years when most sporting activities had ceased. To be sure they were not championship affairs but they were competitive, which helped the breed and kept interest alive while offering a diversion during a time when pleasures were few. The backbone of these "clandestine events" was the Scottish Terrier Breeder's and Exhibitor's Association, a group made up of true supporters of the breed. Members of this group with other holdovers from pre-war years formed the small nucleus that was responsible for the rebirth of the breed when hostilities ceased. The success of the venture is apparent and the Scottish Terrier in Britain is once again strong. Ch. Desert Viscountess, bred by A. Brown, was the first post-war titleholder in 1946. Thereafter competition became extremely active for in 1947, 12 Scots claimed the coveted title. Imports from Britain again made their presence felt in the U.S. rings although there is no doubt that American stock had moved forward into full contention with the best Britain now had to offer.

In the late forties a number of new names became prominent on the British scene in addition to some who have been previously mentioned. W.M. Singleton was still active with Chs. Walsing Winning Trick, Walsing Watch Light and Walsing Winoway, as was C. Bremer with Chs. Ortley Monty, Ortley Simon and others. The Rosehall prefix was also carried over with Chs. Rosehall Edward and Rosehall Toryglen Tam O'Shanter. Names that had not previously been noted included W. Berry's Wyrebury prefix with such dogs as Chs. Wyrebury Woodnymph, Wyrebury Wonder and Wyrebury Witching. The Westpark Scotties came along strong with a host of widely known winners including the great Ch. Westpark Derriford Baffie (a son of Ch. Westpark Romeo), which captured 35 CCs in England and then became a big winner and a great sire in the United States; H. Wright's Woodmansey Winetaster, a recent winner of 16 challenge certificates, together with the Gillsie dogs of

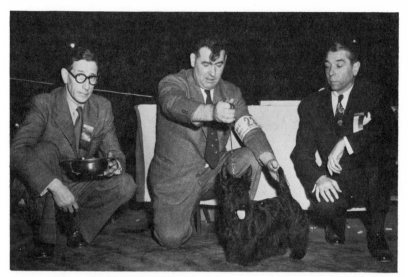

W.M. Singleton of the Walsing prefix made several judging trips to the United States during his lifetime. He is shown here with his BB at the STCA New York Specialty in 1949, Ch. Independent Ben, owned by Joseph Kelly and handled by Jimmy Murphy. Club President Charles Werber (right) looks on.

May 28, 1949 was a great day in the history of the Scot. On this day Mrs. John G. Winant's Ch. Walsing Winning Trick of Edgerstoune was BIS at the great Morris and Essex event under Mrs. David Wagstaff. Mrs. Geraldine R. Dodge, (center) presents the BIS trophy to handler Phil Prentice.

Eng. Ch. Kennelgarth Viking, memorable English stud.

Eng. Ch. Kennelgarth King of Scots at over eight years.

Messrs. Gill and McShane that have included a host of good ones including Ch. Gillsie Principal Girl and Ch. Gillsie Starturn. Add the Desco Scots of Mrs. L.J. Dewar, Newcastle-on-Tyne, who is currently (1979) the president of the Scottish Terrier Club of England and a strong supporter of the breed since about 1934, and one will gain a useful perspective of some of the many individuals who have been active over many years. The Kennelgarth establishment of Miss Betty Penn-Bull also began in the thirties with a bitch, Kennelgarth Greena by Ch. Albourne Admiration. The effort grew and the dog, Heather Herald (Heather Realization ex Heather Louise) was purchased from Chapman. He proved to be a worthy investment for he sired Kennelgarth Blacksmith who is behind much of the present-day stock. After the close of the war, Kennelgarth thrived and challenge certificates began to come its way. Since then, many titleholders have been bred and owned including the first champion, Kennelgarth Mallich, a Heather Herald granddaughter bred by Mrs. Owen. Some of the homebreds include Chs. Kennelgarth Great Scot, Kennelgarth Eros, Kennelgarth Sharon, Kennelgarth Venus and, of course, the great Ch. Kennelgarth Viking (1959-1971) by Eros ex Ch. Kennelgarth Gleam and linebred five times to Kennelgarth Blacksmith. Viking sired a host of titleholders including Chs. Brackenscroft Rye and Dry, Gillsie Starturn and the great Ch. Gaywyn Viscountess. He was surely one of the leading studs of his day and will go down in history as a truly great sire. Of more recent vintage one finds Chs. Kennelgarth King of Scots, Kennelgarth King of Diamonds, Kennelgarth Edrick and Kennelgarth Knight Errant among others. Indeed, today the kennel is just as active as ever and one discovers that Kennelgarth entries are always a challenge in the ring. Miss Penn-Bull has always preferred "blacks" and her strain has maintained excellent coat texture, something that is often absent in this attractive color.

We first visited the Gaywyn Kennels of Mr. and Mrs. H.F. Owen in the fall of 1964 (before it moved to the present, larger quarters) and were amazed to see such a compact establishment so well stocked with top dogs. At that time the roll included Chs. Gaywyn Emperor, Gaywyn Viscountess and Gaywyn Titania. After going over many of the dogs, Mr. Owen opened every stall and some 19 Scots came into the limited floor space to greet us en masse. There was no bickering,

Eng. Ch. Kennelgarth
Edrick.

Eng. Ch. Kennelgarth
Deborah.

Eng. Ch. Kennelgarth
King of Diamonds.

much less fighting and a sea of wagging tails told the story of the temperament at Gaywyn. Of course, the Owens are not newcomers to the breed. Aided by their two daughters, Susan and Catharine (Katie), they have been highly successful for some 25 years although Mrs. Owen had her first Scot in 1937. The initial titleholder bred by the establishement was Kennelgarth Mallich who was made up in 1952 (owned by Betty Penn-Bull) and since then the effort has grown steadily and in the doing, achieved success and international acclaim. Today, it ranks with the best in the breed.

The initial champion owned by the establishment was Ch. Gaywyn Viscountess. After this accomplishment, success was large and today there have been some 25 English champions owned and/or bred at Gaywyn. Among the more widely known Scots in this effort one finds the aforementioned Viscountess, and Chs. Gaywyn Kingson, Leilam, Megan, Matico and of course, Gaywyn Likely Lad who captured some 27 certificates during his career. Subsequently he came to the United States where he became a big winner. The Owens are widely known in America from their imports and because both daughters have been over for extended periods while Mrs. Owen has judged here several times.

Katie and Susan Owen have always been interested in dogs and their sojourns in America allowed them to observe American procedures and techniques of working with fine dogs. In fact, Katie was with the late Betty Malinka at Sandoone for nearly a year. Susan is now married to John S. Gaskell who was also interested in Scottish Terriers and was already breeding and showing under the Mayson prefix. In fact, his initial titleholder was Ch. Gillson Serenade folowed by Ch. Mayson Tommy Toff. Since that time, with the help of his wife, Mr. Gaskell has produced a number of top Scotties and the prefix has become a real challenge in any company. Their success is evident when one considers the dogs that have gained titles, including, Chs. Mayson Swansong, Jennifers Delight of Mayson, Mayson Morag, Gaywyn Landmark and Mayson Canasta, a big winner in 1979. The rather rapid success of this relatively new establishment reflects the life-long experience in the breed by its young owners.

Mrs. Elizabeth Meyer of Hatfield, Herts, has a very prominent post-war kennel at Reanda. Here a steady stream of good ones has been bred and many of these have also been sold in the U.S. Most

Eng. Ch. Gaywyn Viscountness with Frank Butler Memorial Trophy.

Eng. Ch. Gaywyn Wicked Lady.

Eng. Ch. Gaywyn Kingson.

Eng. Ch. Gosmore Eilburn Miss Hopeful, owned by Mrs. Audrey Dallison, was England's top-winning show dog of all breeds for 1968.

Eng. Ch. Mayson Monopoly, owned and bred by Mr. and Mrs. John S. Gaskell, was chosen best Terrier at the 1981 Crufts show by judge Miss Linda Beak. He was handled by Mrs. Gaskell to this outstanding win.

will recall such dogs as Chs. Reanda Rheola and Reanda Rhee, which made their U.S. titles quite easily. Rhee was out of Reanda Rosita, which whelped nine titleholders, a record for the time. Rosita's granddam, Reanda Medwal Marchioness, was the foundation of this fine kennel and her name will be noted in the background of some 23 titleholders bred by Mrs. Meyer. In addition Mrs. Meyer has had a host of toppers in Britain headed by Ch. Reanda Roger Rough, which ruled the boards for several years beginning in about 1957-58 and ended his brilliant career with 25 challenge certificates and a best of breed at Crufts. Other widely known Reanda champions include Reanda Rio Rita, Reanda Rory, Reanda Rosalina and Reanda Raith, to name a few from this prolific breeding establishment. There was Ch. Reanda Ringold, with many challenge certificates and a best in show at Paignton to his credit and more recently, Ch. Reanda River Queen, a 1978 winner. Mrs. Meyer's kennel is very active in terms of exports and Reanda Scots may be discovered winning in many countries around the world.

Reaching into Scotland, the widely known Viewpark establishment of Mr. and Mrs. Archie McLaren, near Glasgow is prominent and rather widely known in America. The McLarens' daughter, Carol frequently handles the dogs to perfection and with great success. Among their many big winners are Chs. Viewpark Dictator, Truly Fair, Anna, Dana, Matador, Vanna, Viewpark Vintner and many more including the memorable Ch. Viewpark Red Hackle. Several of the aforementioned have come to these shores and have had outstanding success in the ring.

Another British fancier who owned dogs of great importance to the breed is Mrs. Audrey Dallison. Her Gosmore kennels have long been known for top show dogs of many breeds. In Scottish Terriers, she owned two that became top show dog of the year. These were Chs. Gosmore Eilburn Miss Hopeful and Gosmore Eilburn Admaration. Both dogs were bred by Mrs. M. Punton (Eilburn). Another big winner owned by Mrs. Dallison was Ch. Gosmore Gillson Highland King, bred by Mr. and Mrs. A. Gill. These three dogs together with many others were flawlessly handled by Vince Mitchell. Highland King and Admaration both came to America where they continued their winning ways for the Clive Pillsburys.

Mrs. Maureen Micklethwaite's Glenecker Kennels near Malvern

Eng. Ch. Reanda Roger Rough, a big winner.

Eng. Ch. Reanda Ringold.

Ch. Viewpark Vintner.

Ch. Gosmore Eilburn Admaration, bred by Mrs. M. Punton and owned by Mrs. Dallison, was England's top Terrier for 1967. He was ultimately purchased by the Clive Pillsburys and continued winning in the United States.

Eng. Ch. Mayson Kandida (Eng. Ch. Mayson Monopoly ex Mayson Kizzy) was the top-winning Scottish Terrier bitch in England for 1980.

is another successful effort. It was begun in 1958 with the foundation bitch, Glenlyon Merryanne, who when bred to Eckersley Eros produced Glenecker Foxhunter. Foxhunter, in turn, sired Chs. Glenecker Golden Nob and Glenecker Fancy Lad. Her first titleholder was, however, a homebred bitch, Ch. Glenecker Golden Girl, by Ch. Glenview Silver Gilt, who qualified for her title in 1966. Interestingly enough, Golden Girl was the last Wheaten (to date) to become a champion in Britain. Mrs. Micklethwaite has a strong interest in this attractively-colored strain and is breeding to maintain its existence and quality at this time.

Other champions bearing the Glenecker prefix include, Chs. Glenecker Jeremy Whu, a strong stud force, and Glenecker Allinone, a dog by Jeremy Whu who also sired Ch. Brio West Side Story. Jeremy Whu's grandson, Ch. Glenecker Danny Boy is one of the most recent champions from this small, select kennel that breeds a type satisfying to the owner's eye. As with most English dogs, Glenecker exhibits are always shown by their owner.

One of the most recent success stories, is the rise of Mrs. N. Holland's Noonsun establishment. Begun about 1967 at Hyde, Cheshire, with a puppy named Noonsun Pride, who also became its first champion, the kennel has grown and prospered amazingly over the past six or seven years. In addition to Pride, such Scots as Chs. Noonsun Merry Monarch, Noonsun Mark, Noonsun New Seeker and Nanette of Noonsun, top winning Scot in Britain for 1977, have brought the establishment consistent notice. Noonsun dogs have always done well abroad with several making their titles on the continent. Other standouts include Noonsun Holly, best at the 1979 Club show as well as Noonsun Marksman already on his way, while Ch. Noonsun Mark was adjudged best at the 1978 Specialty event.

Indeed, if this small but select effort continues to breed with its past success, it will long be among the breed leaders. Mrs. Holland has combined the efforts of established kennels such as Kennelgarth, Gillson and Gaywyn to reach her winning combination. Chs. Kennelgarth Viking, Gillson Grandiloquence and Gaywyn Emperor together with his son Joel appear in the extended pedigrees of many Noonsun winners. Nanette is an interesting example of strong line breeding and shows the great stud force, Ch. Kennelgarth Viking, on both sides of her pedigree. Mrs. Holland, as with many Britishers,

Eng. Ch. Glenecker
Jeremy Whu, winner of 10
CCs and the sire of Ch.
Glenecker All In One and
Ch. Brio West Side Story.

Eng. Ch. Glenecker
Danny Boy.

Ch. Glenecker Golden
Nob, like Jeremy has 10
CCs to his credit. He is also
a Group winner at cham-
pionship shows.

Eng. Ch. Nanette of Noonsun.

Noonsun Marksman and Eng. Ch. Noonsun New Seeker flank some symbols of the success of Mrs. N. Holland's Noonsun establishment.

shows and conditions her own dogs and obviously does a fine job as evidenced by the Noonsun win record.

There are, of course, others distinguished by their great, long term interest in the breed. Miss Jane Miller is one such and her Brio Scots have been a real threat in the ring for many years. Chs. Brio Cabin Boy, Call Me Madam, Chief Barker, Fair and Square and Brio·West Side Story are part of a steady stream of winners emanating from this establishment. There should be many more on the horizon as the operation is quite active.

The Glenview Kennels of A.W. Gee was another postwar effort that had great success. Chs. Glenview Idealist, Golden Disc and Merry Princess are a few of its toppers. The name gained prominence in America in view of dogs exported including Ch. Glenview Grand Duke. In this same connection, R.H. McGill's Glendoune Kennels have also exported some important Scots to America including Chs. Glendoune Gaytime, Gaibonnie and Gwenda. Additionally, Glendoune dogs have done their share of winning in England. Harold and Freda Wright's Woodmansey dogs have been on the scene for many years; their Chs. Stonemoor Prudence and Woodmansey Gosmore Royal King are two recent winners. J. Jeff's Penvale Scottish Terriers have also gained good notices over the many years past.

Among a host of other successful breeder-exhibitors such names as Joe Dodgson (Tiddly-Mount), Mrs. F.M. Sheppard (Tadwick), Mrs. K. Smead (Jetscot), Mr. and Mrs. R.A. Bowles (Boswell), Mrs. Dorothy Standen (Tambrae) and Mr. and Mrs. A. Gill (Gillson) come to mind immediately to augment a long list of active dedicated breeder-exhibitors of the Scottish Terrier.

Last but not least is the Bardene Kennels of Mr. Walter Palethorpe in Derbyshire, which will go down in history since Mr. Palethorpe has the knack of breeding toppers. Ch. Bardene Boy Blue sent to the U.S. several years ago was not bred by Palethorpe, but he has made a name for Bardene by winning well all over the country and climaxing the run with best of breed at Westminster in 1964. To date, however, the greatest accomplishment of Mr. Palethorpe's was the breeding of the magnificent Ch. Bardene Bingo. This dog burned up the shows in England and continued the same pace in the

Eng. & Am. Ch. Bardene Bingo, bellwether of Carnation Farms Kennels.

Ch. Anstamm Dark Venture.

U.S. after his purchase by Carnation Farms in 1964. He was the winner of many best in shows, including Westminster in 1967.

We were fortunate to be present at the 1962 National Terrier show at Leicester when Bingo was but an 11-month-old puppy. He cleaned the boards in the breed and went on to best in show over the top Terriers of England. The dog was a sensation; he looked beautiful at that age, and maturity delivered all his youthful promise. In due course, Bingo sired many top dogs on both sides of the ocean — the ultimate measure of a great dog.

Many other British Kennels bear mention but space limits this short review and those that have been chosen are best known to me. It may be said that the Scottish Terrier had made an all-the-way comeback in Britain after the disastrous period of the war. From the line-up now offered, there will be no dearth of good stock from across the sea in future years.

Ashley Charley, a Scottie of 1884.

Tiree, the first American champion, 1898.

6

The Early Scottish Terrier in America

THE advent of the Scottish Terrier in America was about coincidental with that of other early Terrier breeds. To John Naylor of Mount Forest (Chicago area), Illinois, goes the honor of introducing the Scot to this country. In the 1883 records show that he exhibited such dogs as Tam Glen, Heather and Bonnie Bell in classes for "Rough-haired Terriers." In 1885 Naylor registered the first Scottish Terrier in Volume 2 of the *National American Kennel Club Stud Book*, forerunner of the *American Kennel Club Stud Book*. The dog, named Prince Charlie, was assigned #3310. He was by Billy out of Lady, whelped in April 1881, and bred by D. O'Shea of London, Ontario, Canada, indicating that the breed was possibly established above the border before its entry into the United States. The English import, Queen Lilly, #3311, registered by Naylor at the same time as Prince Charlie, was whelped January 20, 1881, and was sired by King out of Lady Blossom.

The above information disagrees with some other authors who credit the first registration in this country to O.P. Chandler's Dake,

#3688 in the now defunct *American Kennel Register*, a competitive registry to the *National American Kennel Club Stud Book*. Dake was not registered until 1886, about one year after Prince Charlie. It is interesting to note, however, that Dake was sired by Naylor's Tam Glen out of Queen Lilly, which, as noted above, was imported and registered by Naylor. From these particulars there seems very little basis for dispute that Naylor should be credited with bringing the breed to this country.

While no great amount of information is available concerning Naylor's activities, we do know that he imported and showed extensively and that he bred a number of Scottish Terriers in the years following their introduction into this country. Such dogs as Glenlyon (a semi-erect eared one), whelped in 1879 and brought over some time thereafter, Glengarry and Rosie, followed by the homebred litter of Dunbar, Fannie Fern and Gypsy Queen are all found in early records, with the last three exhibited extensively during the 1887 show season.

In spite of his activity, Naylor failed in his efforts to popularize the Scottie and interest in the breed was slight. In fact, the class for "Scotch and hard-coated Terriers" at New York in 1888 failed to secure a single entry. A great improvement came about when several new establishments entered the field shortly afterward. The most successful of these was the Wankie Kennels of Messrs. Henry Brooks and Oliver Ames of Boston, Massachusetts. These fanciers purchased a number of top dogs that made competition interesting for all. Among their acquisitions were Chs. Kilroy, Kilcree, Culblean, and later Tiree and Rhuduman. Of this group, Ch. Tiree proved to be the gem and was certainly worth every cent paid for him. It is said that he won the special for best dog in show at Philadelphia in 1893, although the show catalogue does not list the award. If this is true, Tiree was the first of the breed to capture a best in show in the United States. In 1898, at the age of nine, he completed his U.S. title and became the first U.S. Scottish Terrier champion. Bred by Capt. Wetherall and whelped on May 16, 1889, Tiree was sired by Eng. Ch. Alister out of Coll; these two were half-brother and sister. To Henry Brooks goes the honor of being the first American to breed a U.S. titleholder: Ch. Wankie Diana, whelped in 1892 and sired by Kildee ex Flegg Thistledown. She completed her championship in

1898. Her pedigree is of great interest since Eng. Ch. Alister, by Rambler, was her double grandsire while her paternal grand-dam, Eng. Ch. Ailsa II, was also sired by Rambler. Thus three of her four great-grandsires were the same dog, indicating an early and successful use of intensive line breeding.

By 1895 the Scottish Terrier entry at New York had risen to an all time high of 39, and the breed's show classification that year included the *first* American-bred classes for any breed. Sixteen of the entries came from the Wankie Kennels while seven were from James L. Little's Newcastle Kennels of Brookline, Massachusetts. This was a new and large establishment that through the years registered hundreds of Scotties. Little's big winner of the day was Bellingham Baliff, which made his title in 1899 to become the fifth AKC titleholder in the breed. Baliff was by Whinstone out of a Dundee bitch. The efforts of Little's kennels contributed much to the fancy for many years to come. He imported the great Ch. Ashley Crack, which finished the same year as Baliff, in addition to many others, and he ran the kennel personally until about 1914 when his son, Dr. C.C. Little, took over.

In spite of the upsurge of interest caused by the advent of these newcomers, the fortunes of the Scottish Terrier once again began to wane and competition became difficult to find. Mr. Brooks retired from active participation followed by Mr. Ames in about 1899; this closed the once dominant Wankie Kennels. Some of the slack was taken up by Mrs. Jack Brazier (Craigdarroch Kennels), who owned such dogs as Ch. Heworth Merlin, Ch. Silverdale Queen and Ch. The Laird; Mrs. G.S. Thomas (Brandywine Kennels), who owned the imported half-brother–half-sister team of Chs. Brandywine Jock and Brandywine Jean; Mrs. E.S. Woodward (Sandown Kennels), with Chs. Sandown Garnett, a homebred, and Sandown Heather; and Mrs. H.T. Foote, all of whom showed along the line with Mrs. Brazier taking the lead. In fact, her great little dog Ch. The Laird, whelped in 1901 and imported by George Thomas, dominated the breed for four straight years at Westminster. He was said to have been a grand animal and the best exhibited in the breed until that time and had much to do with the public acceptance of the Scottie to prove an old adage:

Guid gear goes in mickle bundles.

91

Concurrent with the demise of the great Wankie Kennels, a newcomer was seen at the shows. He was Dr. Fayette Ewing of near St. Louis (Kirkwood and Webster Groves), Missouri. Although his interest began in about 1897 when he imported Romany Ringlet, he did not come into big time competition until 1899 when he exhibited the aforementioned Ringlet and the import Loyne Ginger at New York. Ginger gave early evidence of Dr. Ewing's lifetime interest in wheatens and finished her title requirements the following year, to become the seventh American titleholder and the *first* American wheaten champion in the breed. In spite of Dr. Ewing's early efforts, the shows still suffered from small entries and apparent apathy among the fancy. However, Dr. Ewing became the "spark plug" needed to bring about a change for the better. The Scottish Terrier specialty club that had been formed in 1885 was revitalized and in 1900 became the Scottish Terrier Club of America with Ewing as its secretary. This brought together a wide cross-section of Scottie fanciers who now had the interest to work toward a common goal, the good of the breed. The club became a member of the American Kennel Club the same year.

Dr. Ewing was active until about 1947, when he retired from direct participation and ended a glorious half-century in the breed. The kennels, then located in Louisiana, were continued by the family with good success. In fact, the import, Ch. Wyrebury Wrangler made an excellent record in the ring and finished his title in 1955, while the imports Chs. Nosegay Napier and Nosegay Mistress Riverside, both by Eng. Ch. Wyrebury Wilwyn, a Wrangler son, made their titles in 1957 along with a homebred, Ch. Nosegay McDuff.

During his long and active association with the Scotsman, Dr. Ewing imported scores of English champions and was responsible for about as many homebreds. He wrote the first expansive American book on the breed in 1931 which still remains a classic. In addition, he advised fanciers regarding breed happenings through a monthly column carried by one of the leading magazines. As previously noted, Dr. Ewing always had a strong interest in the wheaten. After Loyne Ginger, his next widely publicized import was Glencannie Gingerbread. When exhibited in New York about 1931 he caused quite a stir but did not win. Through the years many others, such as Polhill Pilgrim, Nosegay Buckwheat and Nosegay Lemon Lily, etc., were brought out, and these with their get were used successfully in the breeding programs of Nosegay and other kennels interested in the wheaten. Dr. Ewing will always be remembered as a benefactor of the breed and a champion of the wheaten Scottie. The wheaten Scotsman is discussed in greater depth in the chapter to follow where some more contemporary breeders interested in the color are noted together with a listing of some of their dogs.

In 1906, a large kennel, destined to be highly successful, began operations at Bernardsville, New Jersey. It was the Walescott establishment of Francis G. Lloyd. A steady influx of top imports together with the application of sound breeding techniques provided a host of dogs capable of holding their own in any company. By 1910, Ch. Walescot Invader, known in England as Ch. Clonmel Invader, was the big winner for the kennel. His most important triumph was Best of Breed at the first Specialty show of the Scottish Terrier Club of America. Held at Greenwich, Connecticut on May 28, 1910 with George Mortimer judging. The show had an entry of 61. It was held in conjunction with the national specialties of the Welsh and the West Highland White Terrier Clubs.

The spotlight was taken from Walescott, for a time at least, when in 1911 a 3½ year-old Scot named Ch. Tickle 'Em Jock went best in show at Westminster. This first such triumph for the Scottish Terrier helped breed popularity immeasurably. Jock, owned by Andrew Albright, Jr. of Newark, New Jersey, had been purchased in London the year before for a paltry $500. Jock once sired three champions in a single litter but his accomplishment at Westminster was the feat for which he will always be remembered.

The following year, 1912, found Walescott regaining much of its prestige, and by 1914 the kennel frequently dominated important shows along the East coast. Its chief competition came from the aforementioned Newcastle Kennels, which still showed sporadically, the Earlybird Kennels of W.T. Stern, together with a host of individuals including Henry Bixby (Boglebrae) and Caswell Barrie (Ballantrae), both of the latter widely known in the breed. The Earlybird Kennels of W.T. Stern, New York, housed a host of great Scots including Ch. Earlybird Romany Olivia, Ch. Earlybird Troubadour and Ch. Bapton Beryl, one of the great show bitches of the times. The success of the kennels was aided by Bert Hankinson, who

93

was brought over around 1912 from the Bapton Kennels as kennel manager. He stayed with Earlybird until about 1917, when activity slacked off, and then went into Mr. Lloyd's employ.

It was not unusual for Walescott to bring from 10 to 25 entries to Westminster, no great problem with a kennel census of around 75. In 1918, for example, George Thomas was on the woolsack with some 40 entries to pass on, and 11 of them belonged to Walescott. The winning dog that year was Ch. Walescott Albourne Crow, a repeat from 1917, with Walescott Whim going reserve. Whim was one of a litter by Ch. Walescott Maister Wullie ex Merlewood Merle whelped September 1, 1916; it also included Walescott Wag and Walescott Winkie, all three eventually becoming champions. Wullie himself was a homebred by Walescott Daredevil ex Ch. Walescott Shady Lady. Many other great ones came from the kennels with some 17 eventually claiming the title.

After Mr. Lloyd's sudden death in 1920, Walescott was disbanded and the breed lost a successful and constant supporter. Lloyd was at one time president of the Scottish Terrier Club of America, and a perpetual Memorial Trophy in his name is still the most important of all club offerings.

Three other fanciers who were active before 1920 deserve mention because of their substantial contribution to the breed: Miss Margaret Brigham, Sherwood Hall and R.M. Cadwalader, Jr., who operated the Fairwold Kennels at Fort Washington, Pennsylvania. The importation of Ch. Albourne Beetle from Cowley was a fortunate stroke, for Fairwold benefited from this dog's efforts and was a strong contender for many years.

Thus ends the early history of the breed and its supporters in the United States. Many other persons had their share in laying the foundation of sound breeding techniques and proper ethics, but those noted here surely deserve special mention for their efforts. Had it not been for them, the breed may well have fallen out of favor and into oblivion. That it became perennially more virile is evidence that their efforts were not in vain. We of today owe to those of yesterday a large vote of thanks for a job well done.

7

The Modern Scottish Terrier in America

THE preceding chapter delineates the early activities of individuals and kennels that supported the Scotsman in America from its introduction to about the year 1920. This chapter will begin with happenings after that date until the present day. There will be some overlap since the interest of a few fanciers embraced parts of both periods. In any event this era is an important span of years that has meant a great deal to the breed.

After World War I we find establishments that were active before the War still breeding and exhibiting dogs. Some of these will be scanned more thoroughly since they gained in stature as time went on. Included among this select group were the strong contenders, Caswell Barrie, Henry Bixby and R.M. Cadwalader, Jr. Mr. Barrie's Ballantrae establishment had such Scots as Ch. Heather Venture O'Ballantrae and Ch. Ballantrae Wendy in the ring, while Bixby's Boglebrae Kennel was exhibiting Ch. Boglebrae Muskrat and Ch. Ornsay Autocrat, to name two. Bixby will also be remembered because of his many years of association with the American Kennel

Club as its Executive Vice President. Cadwalader's Fairwold complex was previously mentioned because of Ch. Albourne Beetle, but the years greatly improved its stature with such Scots as Ch. Fairwold Albourne Rocket, Ch. Fairwold Ornsay Bill, Ch. Fairwold Osmond Lily and Ch. Fairwold Plaid, a homebred by Beetle out of Clonmel Plaid. The kennels remained active well into the 1930's.

The modern Scottie has these and their predecessors to thank together with that knowledgeable breeder, Frank Spiekerman (Hitofa Kennels), who owned many toppers, including Ch. Heather Essential, Ch. Heather Aristocrat and Ch. Hitofa Chief, and Prentice Talmadge's Bentley Kennels, which imported many good ones including Ch. Albourne Adair, about 1922. Adair was, of course, the keystone of both the Necessity and the Barty lines through his two sons Chs. Albourne MacAdair and Albourne Scot, respectively. When this kennel was dispersed, Adair went to Robert McKinven's Ardmore Kennels near Detroit. Here he was used with great success on many of the Ardmore bitches to produce such get as Ch. Ardmore Wallace, the immortal Ch. Ardmore Skipper and the brood Ardmore Jewel. She was bred twice with great results. The first time when put to her half-brother Skipper, she produced a bitch named Ch. Ardmore Keepsake; the second time, bred to Ch. Ardmore Legacy, an Adair grandson, she produced Ch. Ardmore Toddler.

McKinven did not lose his advantage and bred Toddler to Keepsake, and the dog Ch. Ardmore Royalist resulted. He was a great winner and with a triple cross of Adair blood in his veins was another bit of proof, if proof be needed, that line breeding is the surest means of obtaining results. Bob McKinven retired from active participation about 1937 after breeding some 14 champions, and the kennel was carried on by his son Charles, who is still breeding Scotties with the Ardmore prefix, to make the establishment one of the oldest in the breed in this country. McKinven's stock was always in demand and his Ch. Ardmore Rowdy went to Mrs. Clarence Stanley's Eagle Creek Kennels at Indianapolis. Mrs. Stanley was active during the twenties and thirties and had many other good ones including Chs. Eagle Creek Leebie, Bellstane Queen and Eng. Ch. Albourne Royalist among others.

Returning to other fanciers during the twenties we find Jock McOwen of Mine Brook; John Goudie of Cedar Pond, who always

Ch. Wee Swagger, owned by George P. Tilley.

Claddoch Necessity, owned by John W. Hillman.

has been able to breed a good one; the late Ben Brown, a widely known West Coast handler who came from Dundee, Scotland as a youth and imported many fine Scots from his grandfather's Abertay establishment for clients, Mr. and Mrs. Cecil Jelley (Balgay Kennels) including, Chs. Abertay Harry, Abertay Hawk and Abertay Scot who became the foundation of a highly successful breeding program that produced Chs. Balgay Barrister, Baroness and Drummer Boy among a host of others; Edward Danks, a long time breeder and judge and a lifetime fancier of the breed; Dr. and Mrs. Charles Lynch of Red Gauntlet fame; Bert Hankinson and his Scotsholme Kennels at Basking Ridge, New Jersey; Mr. and Mrs. H. Alvin McAleenan, who owned the Vigal Kennels with a topper in Ch. Goldfinder's Babe and still strongly interested in the breed; and of course, Mr. and Mrs. E.F. Maloney, who owned and operated the Goldfinder Kennels for so many years.

Maloney was one in a million when it came to breeding prowess. The list of good ones he owned and bred seems never ending. Always operating a small establishment, he repeatedly came up with toppers. He owned the great Ch. Heather Gold Finder, a sterling name in the breed and the sire of the aforementioned Goldfinder's Babe, together with some 18 other champions. Possibly his most successful show dog was a homebred, Ch. Goldfinder's Admiral, which was shown by Johnny Murphy during the early fifties and made a great name for himself. Maloney was active until his death and will always be remembered as an astute breeder and a staunch supporter of the breed.

This about ends the decade of the twenties, when the Scottie became of age and improvement was accomplished by a greater distribution of interest than ever before. The thirties opened without fanfare, but little did proponents of the breed know that the next ten years were to be the most productive in its history. In spite of the depression, which thwarted everything else, the Scottish Terrier enjoyed its greatest moments. The ten-year span was the spawning ground for more strong kennels than any other time in the long history of the breed. The period found the Scottie reaching its peak in representation. In 1933, 1936, 1937 and 1938 the breed placed third in numbers registered among all breeds of dogs on the American Kennel Club rolls. Numerically, too, the breed reached its pin-

Left to right: Ed Johnson, Edward Maloney and Johnny Murphy.

Edward Danks (left) was a devoted, lifelong fancier of the Scottish Terrier. He is shown here awarding BB at the STC of Pennsylvania to Ch. Barberry Knowe Merrymaker, owned by Mr. and Mrs. Charles C. Stalter.

nacle. In 1936, a total of 8,359 dogs were registered, the largest number in Scottie history. Compare this with the 1980 figure of 6,334; thus one can readily understand how the breed has slipped. Indeed, this was a golden era for the Scottish Terrier and one that will not soon be forgotten. Carlyle once said: "Popularity is as a blaze of illumination," and such was the case here.

So many fine kennels got their start in the thirties that it would be difficult to list them all. Few still remain, so these will be considered first, with those that have closed to be mentioned later.

At the start of the decade we find that the Barberry Knowe Kennel of Mr. and Mrs. Charles C. Stalter bears early mention, since it was begun in 1929 and became one of the strongest show kennels in the breed in the United States. Situated in Northern New Jersey for nearly 50 years, it was started when Mrs. Stalter bought her husband a Scottie for Christmas. The dog, Diehard Robin, matured into a likely looking youngster. For a lark, the Stalters decided to show him at Englewood, New Jersey in 1930. He won his class, and as is the case with so many others, the Stalters were bitten by the show bug. Although Robin never quite made the grade, the Stalters were sufficiently interested to return to William McBain (Diehard Kennels) and purchase another male puppy, Diehard Reveller, sired by Ch. Heather Reveller of Sporran out of an imported bitch, Glenisla Grizelda. They brought him out in 1932 and by July of the following year the Stalters had their first champion. The next purchase was a bitch, Caenmohr Cora, which proved a worthy investment when, bred to Ch. Diehard Reveller, she produced Ch. Barberry Knowe Reveller, their first homebred titleholder.

Since that time Barberry Knowe has been a name with which to reckon at the shows all over the eastern section of the country. The Stalters had a host of good ones and more than their share of great ones. Their Ch. Barberry Knowe Barbican was one of the leading winners during the period of the early fifties when Scottie competition was extremely difficult. More lately, their Ch. Carmichael's Fanfare was one of the top Scots for the years 1963 and 1964, climaxing her already illustrious career with best in show at Westminster in 1965 to become the fourth of the breed to make this difficult and coveted win. She was wisely retired after the accomplishment.

From the beginning of their operations until early in 1965, the

100

Barberry Knowe Rascal.

Ch. Barberry Knowe Babrican, a pacesetter for the breed during the early 1950s.

A view of the beautiful lounge at the Stalters' Barberry Knowe Kennels. This was one of the oldest and most distinguished Scottish Terrier Kennels in the world. It was the home of many great homebreds, imports and others that brought great honors back to their home base.

Ch. Barberry Knowe Barbican with Phil Prentice, Mrs. John G. Winant and George Hartman, judge, 1950.

Ch. Barberry Knowe Wyndola, owned by Barberry Knowe Kennels and handled by Florence Prentice was best Terrier at Devon 1955 under judge Edward Danks.

Ch. Carmichael's Fanfare winning the Garden, 1965, with Johnny Murphy handling; Robert Kerns, judge, and William Rockefeller awarding the trophy.

Ch. Barberry Knowe Spitfire, owned by Barberry Knowe Kennels and handled by R. Stephen Shaw was best Terrier at the Newtown (Connecticut) KC show under the author.

John P. Murphy, one of the breed's most gifted handlers, with Ch. Carmichael's Fanfare photographed following their great BIS victory at the 1965 Westminster event.

The renown William Prentice of the Barlae prefix passed his talents to his son Phil and daughter Florence. All were superlative terrier people.

Charles Stalter, Florence Prentice with best brace at 1956 Scottish Terrier Club of America being awarded ribbon by the author.

Stalters were fortunate in availing themselves of the knowledge, good counsel, and superlative handling ability of the Prentice family. William (Bill) Prentice, his son Phil, and his daughter Florence were all associated with Barberry Knowe at one time or another and in overlapping periods. The early handling and counsel was done by Bill Prentice, a Scot of great knowledge and good judgment and the owner of Barlae Kennels. When Bill was unable to continue because of other commitments, Phil took over and did a remarkable job. Concurrently, Florence Prentice was kennel manager and private handler for the kennels, continuing in this capacity until her death in 1965. Her knowledge and ability to condition Scotties for show and to bring youngsters along to maturity, as well as her frank and pleasant personal approach, were major factors in the steady success of the establishment. It is difficult to realize that all three Prentices are now gone. All were top dog people; all were superlative Scottie conditioners and handlers. Their passing was a great loss to the breed.

During the period of from about 1960 to 1968, Johnny Murphy, who gained his early training at Chapman's Heather Kennels in Scotland, handled the Barberry Knowe dogs and a fine job he did. The climax of his efforts came in 1965 when he piloted the incomparable Ch. Carmichael's Fanfare to Westminster's top spot. Charles Stalter died in 1968, the same year that Murphy retired from handling to begin his all-too-short judging career. He died in 1973. Steve Shaw assumed the duties of show handler with Miss Kingsbury, who had become kennel manager around 1965 remaining at that post until the kennel closed its doors in New Jersey.

Throughout its long existence, Barberry Knowe bred and/or owned over 100 titleholders that were always threats at any show. In late years some of their top showmen, in addition to Barbican and Fanfare, included such Scots as, Chs. Barberry Knowe Wyndola, Walsing Wild Winter of Barberry Knowe, Barberry Knowe Blizzard, Barberry Knowe Spitfire, Balachan Naughty Gal, Barberry Knowe My Fair Lady and many other fine ones. In 1975, Steve Shaw retired to begin his judging career and Miss Kingsbury assumed the handling chores as well as managing the establishment. On December 30th of the same year, Mrs. Stalter died to end an era. She wisely willed the dogs and the kennel name to Miss Kingsbury who con-

105

tinues the operation from a new location at Canadensis, Pennsylvania. Indeed, Barberry Knowe is a name that deserves perpetuation in memory of the Stalters — fine people who were always a credit to the breed.

For a good many years another kennel of long standing that has shown to advantage is the Shieling establishment of Mr. and Mrs. T. Howard Snethen. Getting its start in Wisconsin, the dogs were moved to Allison Park (Pittsburgh area), Pennsylvania soon after its beginning, where they remained for many years. Today, the Shieling Scotties are housed at DeWittville, N.Y.

The most important fact about this group is the absence of professional help in the exhibition and grooming of its dogs. Mr. Snethen has always done the trimming and handling, and his artistry in doing up a Scot rivals that of the best professional. He is also a great ring competitor. The kennel, like many others gained its start through a top brood bitch, Dark Maid. She whelped several of the early titleholders and got the show on the road. One of the first toppers bred by Shieling was the dog Ch. Shieling's Stylist. He was followed by Ch. Shieling's Designer, Ch. Shieling's Flash, Ch. Shieling's Signature, Ch. Shieling's Masterkey and Ch. Shieling's Insignia, among many others. All of these were homebreds and all won best in show honors with Mr. Snethen on the other end of the lead. Signature had the added honor of topping all breeds at Westminster in 1945 to become the second Scotsman to turn the trick. This was a great achievement for man and dog, for seldom does this prize go to a dog handled by an amateur.

In more recent years, the kennel has imported some good ones including Ch. Reanda Rheola and Ch. Glenview Grand Duke; both have done extremely well. Soon, more homebreds appeared at the shows, giving strong accounts of themselves for Shieling. The kennel has bred more than 40 champions and has owned a host of others to make it one of the most successful in the breed.

Another kennel, and one of the most extensive on the West Coast, is the Carnation Farms establishment of E.H. Stuart, at Carnation, Washington. Mr. Stuart's interest in the breed began during the middle twenties while he resided in Wisconsin, through association with Mrs. Marie Stone, Charles Schott, and others. Not until about 1932, however, did a kennel evolve, and this was at its present loca-

Ch. Shieling's Signature winning
Westminster Best in Show, 1945.

```
                                                            Eng. Ch. Heather Ambition
                                        Ch. Heather Independence of E.
                                                            Heather Marina
                    Ch. Heather Criterion
                                                            Eng. Ch. Heather Realisation
                                        Heather Doris
                                                            Albourne Black Tulip
        Ch. Shieling's Salute
                                                            Ch. Drum Major of Docken
                                        Ch. Glencannie Crusader O'Briarcroft
                                                            Eng. Ch. Albourne Red Mary
                    Ch. Shieling's Winsome
                                                            Sandheys Simon of Wotan
                                        Dark Maid
                                                            Wotan's Frost Lassie
CH. SHIELING'S SIGNATURE
(Whelped 5/5/1942                                           Ch. Drum Major of Docken
Breeder: Mr. and Mrs. T. H. Snethen)    Ch. Glencannie Crusader O'Briarcroft
                                                            Eng. Ch. Alnbourne Red Mary
                    Ch. Shieling's Stylist
                                                            Sandheys Simon of Wotan
                                        Dark Maid
                                                            Wotan's Frost Lassie
        Ch. Shieling's Symphony
                                                            Eng. Ch. Heather Fashion Hint
                                        Ch. Walnut Dandy O'Briarcroft
                                                            Eng. Ch. Albourne Braw Lassie
                    Ch. Shieling's Enterprise
                                                            Sandhey's Simon of Wotan
                                        Lucky Nancy
                                                            Wotan's Black Ruby
```

tion. Several top Scots were purchased during the thirties including an import, Ch. Gaisgill Daphne, and two outstanding American-breds in Ch. Goldfinder's Lady and Ch. Quince Hill Brick. The latter sired the kennel's first homebred titleholder in 1938, Ch. Carnation Classic.

Increased exhibition and success came with Bob Bartos, who became manager of the kennel in 1947. One of his first acts was to bring over Ch. Reimill Radiator, a son of Westpark Masterpiece. He was followed a few years later by a half-brother, Ch. Westpark Rio Grande, which sired 12 English and 21 American titleholders to place him high in the lists of great producers. Ch. Westpark Derriford Baffie was the next top import, purchased after he had won an unprecedented 35 challenge certificates in English rings. He proved equally successful in this country, as Bartos piloted him to 50 best of breeds at all-breed shows without a defeat; he went on to best dog in show at 22 of the outings, and he won four specialties as well. His siring ability was also highly commendable, with eight English and 19 American champions to his credit. Many other fine dogs have been inmates of this successful kennel, including particularly Ch. Dorel Black Nugget and Ch. Deephaven Red Seal. Carnation was also the first to have a wheaten good enough to go best in show, this honor won by homebred Ch. Carnation Golden Girl, which topped the Yakima, Washington show in 1951. She was strong in the blood of Heather Asset. Bob Bartos and Carnation Farms reached the pinnacle of achievement in 1967 when the fine import, Ch. Bardene Bingo capped his illustrious career by becoming best in show at Westminster—the fifth Scottish Terrier to claim Westminster's highly-coveted top spot. This triumph surely climaxed the efforts of Carnation Farms Kennels — breeders of over fifty titleholders while owning many more during its existence—a record of which to be proud.

Among the many kennels that were successful in the thirties but no longer active we find the Quince Hill prefix of Dr. and Mrs. Morgan Steinmetz, William Prentice's Barlae Kennels, which began even earlier, and the Kinclaven Kennels of Mrs. Marie Stone of Milwaukee. This last establishment was begun in the late twenties but gained a large measure of its fame in the next two decades. It was closed by the death of its owner which was a great loss to the fancy. Kinclaven produced some three score champions which included

Ch. Deephaven Red Seal.

Ch. Marlu Crusader
Ch. Walsing Warrant
Eng. Ch. Heather Realisation
Eng. Ch. Heather Fashion Hint
Gaisgill Sylvia
Eng. Ch. Walsing Wellborn
Eng. Ch. Malgen Juggernaut
Walsing Waitress

Ch. Marlu Malady
Eng. Ch. Dandy of Docken
Eng. Ch. Heather Fashion Hint
Brilliant of Docken
Roseneath Miss Muffett
Scotshome Humorist
Sandridge Sabula

CH. DEEPHAVEN RED SEAL
(Whelped 6/26/1945
Breeder: Deephaven Kennels)

Ch. Kinclaven Classic
Ch. Kinclaven Tobasco
Heather Asset
Ch. Carioca
Ch. Gleniffer Leading Lady
Eng. Ch. Heather Realisation
Gleniffer Gaiety

Deephaven Mary

Mac's Welton Gold Penny
Deephaven Sir Galahad
Nosegay Buckwheat
Graochen Bittersweet
Mac's Welton Hope
Faraway Sandy of Mt. Tuck
Clarksdale Anne

Ch. Deephaven Red Seal with Bob Bartos and Ch. Carnation Golden Girl with Jane Bartos photographed with judge Derek Rayne at the Eugene KC (Oregon). They were BB and BOS here respectively, but both were BIS winners and Golden Girl was the first wheaten Scot with a top win.

Ch. Reimill Radiator, owned by Carnation Farms, was an influential stud and a good winner. He is shown here winning the Terrier Group at Seattle under the legendary Alva Rosenberg, handler Bob Bartos.

Eng. and Am. Ch. Bardene Bingo, owned by E. H. Stuart, one of the modern greats, was BIS at Westminster 1967 under judge Percy Roberts to cap a brilliant show career. Bingo is shown here immediately following his great triumph with handler Bob Bartos.

the best in show winner Ch. Kinclaven The Stooge, together with Ch. Kinclaven Classic and Ch. Kinclaven Wild Oats, a wheaten but more about him later. In all cases, Mrs. Stone handled her own dogs and was most successful.

Before proceeding with a chronology of the breed I must digress to reach into the history of the wheaten Scottish Terrier. While a few have been mentioned no substantial survey has been offered and, indeed, little may be discovered in the literature concerning this color variation. There is small question that wheatens are better received in America than in Britain where the last wheaten champion was Mrs. Micklethwaite's, Ch. Glenecker Golden Girl who made her title in 1966 becoming only the eighth of the color to gain the title. As previously mentioned, Dr. Ewing showed early interest when he imported a bitch, Loyne Ginger and made her the seventh champion in the breed in 1899 and the first wheaten titleholder. In the ensuing years only a few were noted and there appeared to be small interest in the variation.

In the middle forties, this apathy was dispelled by three ladies who were determined to improve the status of the wheaten Scotsman — Mrs. Constable (Murray), Mrs. Henshaw (Henshaw's) and the aforementioned Mrs. Stone (Kinclaven). The first two collaborated, breeding and exhibiting a number of wheatens with only average success. The ones I observed at the time were poor-headed, weedy and had coats often shot with black hairs. However, in 1946, Mrs. Henshaw bred a bitch that was transferred to Mrs. Constable who named it Murray Rag Doll and it became a champion in 1946. Rag Doll, interestingly enough, traced back to a triple cross of Nosegay Buckwheat, an earlier product of Dr. Ewing's effort. Thereafter, Mrs. Stone, who was one of the top breeders of the time, had success with the likes of Chs. Kinclaven Wild Oats, Kinclaven Ever Amber (first wheaten to win a specialty), Kinclaven Corn Silk and Kinclaven Coq D'or. Wild Oats was a classic Scotsman and did some fine winning while impressing exhibitors and judges alike.

In the same general time frame, there was activity in the Northwest and Carnation Farms was successful in breeding a bitch, Carnation Golden Girl, who was piloted by Bob Bartos to the title and who became the first of the color to capture a best in show award (1951). Two other breeders in the same general area also had inter-

Marie Stone with her great wheaten, Ch. Kinclaven
Wild Oats.

Ch. Murray Rag Doll, owned by Mrs. William Constable and bred by
Mrs. A.M. Henshaw.

113

Ch. Young's Samantha,
with her owner-handler
Elaine Young.

Ch. Kenjo Gold Braid Commander, owned and handled by Kennan Glaser, shown
in a win under John W. Hillman.

est and success; Mrs. W.K. Robertson's Glad-Mac establishment owned and/or bred several good ones including Chs. Cedar Root Gaydes Gold and Glad-Mac's Golden Princess among others while Mrs. Elaine Young had success with four wheaten champions including a standout, Ch. Young's Samantha. Mrs. John Gilkey, operating in Wisconsin, bred and exhibited such wheatens as Chs. Gilkey's Desert Image, Wild Honey and Sugar Time, while Mrs. Ruth Czeskleba, of the Washington, D.C. area, had a good winner in Ch. Ardeecee Wee Bit of Honey. Mrs. Louise Elsworth (Elscot) and the Anthony Stamms (Anstamm) both should be included here as they bred and exhibited wheatens with gratifying success.

In the sixties, the Detroit-based fancier, Peter Babisch bred a bitch, Ch. Yankee Pride Blushing Squaw who was subsequently sold to and shown by John Treleaven of Canada. She caused quite a stir when she captued the points at the 1962 national specialty in New York and continued to win well. Most recently, Ken Glaser (Kenjo) of Michigan bred a dog named Kenjo Gold Braid Commander that completed title requirements in the seventies. He in turn sired a bitch, Ch. Kenjo Little Red Riding Hood. There are undoubtedly others of this attractive color around the land but it is surely a fact that the numbers are small which makes those of championship calibre even less numerous. These remarks are supported by the fact that, to date, there are less than fifty that have made the title. Hopefully fanciers will support the wheaten so that the color may move forward. Genetically, it appears almost impossible to predict wheaten offspring with any degree of certainty from a mating. Seldom do they appear in a litter, so breeding the color requires both dedication and fortitude. One point of importance, a really good wheaten should be the color of ripe wheat and not a light fawn or cream. Dr. Ewing himself said that Scots of the later variants were "neither fish nor fowl," a rather firm statement.

Returning to more familiar colors, two Midwest kennels of the era beginning in the thirties were Briarcroft at Youngstown, Ohio, and Deephaven at Minneapolis, Minnesota. Briarcroft was owned by Dr. F.W. Zimmerman. He, with Clint Schenck of Columbus, who was his inseparable companion at the shows, imported and exhibited a host of great ones. Most came from the aforementioned Sam Bamford's Walnut Kennels in England. He also bred some fine dogs and

Ch. Deephaven Fixed Asset, one of many title holders from T.W. Bennett's successful establishment.

Ch. Hillcote Destiny, a multiple BIS winner bred by John W. Hillman.

showed consistently for many years. He owned Ch. Hillcote Laddie during the period when the dog made history in both ring and breeding pen. Dr. Zimmerman's interests were also captivated by Welsh and Airedale Terriers, although Scots were his last effort before bowing out of competition in the late forties.

The Deephaven Kennels of Mr. T.W. Bennett was an amazingly successful establishment which began in the early thirties to climax an interest in the breed that extended several previous years. Mr. Bennett was fortunate in having Bob Bartos from the beginning until 1947, when he left to join Carnation Farms. The kennel closed its doors about 1950. Top dogs became the order of the day when the bitch Scotsward Romance was purchased at the Morris and Essex show from Mrs. C.B. Ward. She later became the first titleholder for Deephaven. Following closely was the great Ch. Crich Certainty, an import that proved to be a good sire. Thereafter more than 20 titleholders came from Deephaven, including Deephaven Fair Damsel, the first homebred champion, Deephaven Goldust, the Deephaven Honeysuckle, the great show dog, Ch. Deephaven Warspite, and finally Ch. Deephaven Red Seal, sold to Marlu Farms at a year old. This dog became one of the truly great sires of all time. The breeding record of Deephaven was surely exemplified by an inscription on the wall of the kennel lounge, which read, "The Best Is None Too Good."

In addition, some others who began serious efforts during this period include Dr. Flora Pedicord, whose dogs were shown by that old master, Dick Davis; John Hillman, a former judge and the breeder of Ch. Hillcote Laddie. Laddie and his litter brother, Mrs. Henshaw's Ch. Hillcote Essential Knight, sired by Ch. Heather Essential out of Henshaw's Gloaming, a daughter of Ch. Heather Reveller of Sporran. Hillman also bred Ch. Hillcote Destiny which proved to be a big winner. He was by Claddoch Necessity of Briarcroft, another producing son of the incomparable Necessity. Mr. and Mrs. Henry Israel's Paisley Hill Kennels at Dayton also brought out many good ones, including Fashion Favorite and Ch. Marlu Clincher which, guided by Johnny Murphy, made history in the early fifties, while John Kemp of Acton Hill fame with Ch. Acton Hill Interventionist, etc. was a widely known name during the same period.

117

Marguerite Kirmse and some of her Scots with an Irish visitor.

Illustration from a Marguerite Kirmse Christmas card

In the West, the Bryce Gillespie's Bothkennar Kennels merit mention for their excellence and longevity. Begun around 1930 it flourished until its closing after the war, and during this span finished nearly two score champions. One of the most outstanding of these, Ch. Trevone Tartar of Bothkennar, an import, developed into one of the country's top sires. In later years such dogs as Ch. Bothkennar Typesetter and Ch. Bothkennar Kilroy kept the name in the headlines. Returning to Eastern climes, the Glenafton Kennels of Miss Elizabeth Hull flourished for a period of years beginning in the thirties. Jimmy Murphy, Johnny Murphy's brother, was the handler, and his charges included such Scots as Ch. Goldfinder's Lassie, Ch. Walsing Wagtail, Ch. Glenafton Tamara and Ch. Glenafton Goldseeker. The kennels were located at Binghamton, New York in the winter and were taken to the cool shores of Lake Lenape during the hot summer months to assure complete comfort for all inmates.

Another who was quite active in the breed over a long period was Marguerite Kirmse who subsequently became Mrs. George Cole. She began her interest in the early twenties as a partner with the widely known artist, Edwin Megargee using the Tobermory prefix. Miss Kirmse later married George Cole and they moved to Connecticut where she resided for the remainder of her life. George Cole was also active in the breed and at one time was president of the national specialty club. Of course, Marguerite Kirmse is best remembered today for her many appealing etchings of dogs, Scotsmen in particular. Many homes have one or more of these works of art whose execution reflects her knowledge of the breed. In fact, her artistic efforts have done much to further public interest in the breed.

Frank Brumby is now well remembered today as an expert on the breed, but few realize his background extended over a half century in active participation with the Scotsman. He managed, among other kennels, the Hillwood establishment of Mrs. Thomas W. Durant at Roslyn, Long Island during the early thirties, and no expense was spared to import the best as foundation stock. The great Ch. Merlewood Hopeful, which gained her English title in 32 days and her American title in 27 days, was one of these. Others were Ch. Wilfield Necessity, a Heather Necessity son, Albourne Reveller's Lad, Ch. Laurieton Lorraine, Chs. Rookery Doon and Rookery Romance, and Ch. Bramble No Less. Upon reduction of activity at

Hillwood Brumby went to the Braw Bricht Kennels of Mr. and Mrs. Donald Voorhees at Jericho, Long Island, another important establishment that enjoyed a rather brief tenure. The plan of Braw Bricht began in about 1932 when Rogue of Hillwood was purchased. The following year the kennel gained momentum through the purchase of the import, Gleniffer Ideal, from Brumby, who then handled the dogs and became its manager. Later the same year Ortley Angela was brought over and both made their titles, with Angela accomplishing the feat in sensational style at that first five shows.

Flornell Soundman, purchased from Percy Roberts, became the bellwether of the kennel with many best in show awards—eight in one year—while one of the most satisfying wins was the award of best team in show at Westminster in 1934, captured by the quartet of Chs. Gleniffer Ideal, Gleniffer Frivolity, Gleniffer Glad Eye and Ramoan Certainty. The last named did well in the groups and even gained a best in show but was always overshadowed by his more glamorous kennelmate, Soundman. Two other Braw Bricht Scotties that warrant mention in view of their sterling type and ability were Ch. Cedar Pond Chloe, bred by John Goudie, and Ch. Craigieburn Expectation of Sporran.

Most readers today will identify Mr. Voorhees with music rather than Scotties; he was one of the best known conductors, frequently seen on television with his Bell Telephone Orchestra. Braw Bricht is only a memory today, but during the middle 1930's it cut a wide swath in competitive breed activity.

This brings us to three of the largest kennels of the era, two of which continued for many years and actually dominated the breed through long periods. The first was short-lived but nonetheless large and important. This was the Sporran Kennels of author S.S. Van Dine, who wrote many intriguing mystery stories, one of which, *The Kennel Murder Case*, imortalized the Scottie. He was always a dog lover and began to breed seriously as a diversion from his hectic literary life. Sporran was a busy place around 1930 with more than 100 Scotsmen romping around the pens as the owner tried to evolve a plan for breeding dogs in America as well as they did in England. He once said, "We have in the United States, with one or two exceptions, all the best Scottish Terrier sires living," and he added, "A similar statement is true in regard to brood bitches. Yet our Ameri-

120

Ch. Glenafton Tamara and Ch. Walsing Wag Tail.

Ch. Wilfield Necessity.

can-breds are beaten time after time by imported specimens." He concluded, and rightly so, "We have been breeding to champions, not bloodlines." These remarks are reminiscent of similar views expressed by many knowledgeable breeders who decry the novice's desire to breed to the top dog of the year, whether the bitch has the proper bloodlines or not. It also goes back to related advice made by A.G. Cowley and found in the chapter on British Breeders and Kennels.

Van Dine had William Prentice as his handler and manager, the best available. He brought over Ch. Heather Reveller, which gained the "of Sporran" suffix upon his naturalization. Sporran also owned Ornsay Hustler of Diehard, a widely known stud. Reveller made his English title in three consecutive shows at the age of 11 months. In America his accomplishments were just as sensational although more extensive. In three years of exhibition he won the breed 49 times, the group 21 times and best in show ten times. There were only two events at which he failed to place in the group. Only one champion was ever bred with the Sporran prefix, Ch. Sporran Roger, and he was not by the kennel's big dog, Reveller. After Van Dine decided to close his kennel in late 1934, Reveller went to Prentice.

The other two "big" kennels of the era were Edgerstoune and Relgalf. They will be taken up separately and in some detail because of their impact on the breed and the excellence of their activities. One of the largest and more successful kennels in the country began operations in the late twenties when Mrs. Marion Eppley, then Mrs. John G. Winant, started Edgerstoune. In the beginning the inmates were mostly West Highlanders, but in 1934 Scottish Terriers came into the picture. For the remainder of its long and glorious tenure these two Scottish breeds made history, with close to 100 champions being bred or owned from its inception in New Hampshire until its closing at Valley Cottage, New York in 1954.

Edgerstoune obtained the best from England, and these, with proper breeding, brought a host of top homebreds into the fold. Some of the better known imports were Ch. Gleniffer Tid Bit of Edgerstoune, Ch. Heather Resolution of Edgerstoune, Ch. Heather Commodore of Edgerstoune, and the incomparable Ch. Walsing Winning Trick of Edgerstoune. Homebreds were legion and Ch. Edgerstoune Troubadour, by Trick, stands out; he was sold as

S.S. Van Dine (left) with unidentified friends in the early thirties.

Ch. Walsing Winning Trick of Edgerstoune going best in show at Westminster, 1950. Left to right: Phil Prentice, John Cross, George Hartman and Ross Proctor.

Ch. Edgerstoune Troubadour, owned by Dr. and Mrs. W. Stewart Carter, was a great winning son of Ch. Walsing Winning Trick of Edgerstoune. He is shown here in one of his numerous important victories, BIS at Chagrin Valley (Ohio) in 1952 under T.H. Carruthers III, handler Jake Terhune.

youngster, before he became a champion, to Dr. and Mrs. Stewart Carter. Additionally there was Ch. Edgerstoune Pepper, a fine dog that was overshadowed by his more spectacular kennelmate, Trick.

The kennels always had good young stock to replace the class dogs as they completed their titles. This was not happenstance, for Mrs. Eppley used an unusual method to raise her homebreds. Puppies were always an operation unto themselves. Mrs. Fred Leonard had charge of this phase of the work, and her efforts were certainly apparent. The older dogs and show stock were housed in a separate kennel with its own manager, who in most cases was also the show handler. Edgerstoune had the good fortune of having many fine handlers and managers in the persons of Harry Hardcastle, Bob Gorman, Jimmy Murphy, Joe Menary, and Cliff Hallmark. Phil Prentice also handled dogs for the kennel although he never managed its operations. In any event, Mrs. Leonard's concentrated efforts on puppies paid off because the youngsters received more attention, and their dispositions reflected this attention.

Much of the progress made by the kennel can also be attributed to Mrs. Eppley's ability to pick a winner at home or abroad. This was demonstrated by the way she acquired two of her best. When she judged in England, she placed a Westie bitch best in show. Immediately after the judging, she bought her and brought back to this country Ch. Wolvey Pattern of Edgerstoune, which went best in show at Westminster in 1942. Again in England, Mrs. Eppley placed a Scottish Terrier best in show, then bought the dog, Ch. Walsing Winning Trick. Of course, it is history now, but Trick subsequently emulated Pattern and won best in show at Westminster in 1950, when he carried the "of Edgerstoune" suffix to the top.

Before leaving Edgerstoune, a run-down of Winning Trick's record will be of interest, for it is an amazing one that has never been equalled. Shown sparingly with only 40 outings at large shows over a period of about three years, he was never defeated in the breed and only failed to win the group at three events where group competition was offered. At these he was second twice and out of the ribbons the other time. He won best in show 28 times including such affairs as Morris and Essex (1949), Westchester (1949), Westbury (1948 and 1949), and Westminster, Eastern Dog Club and the International, all in 1950. In addition he captured all three specialty events in

Ch. Silvertip of Gedling.

Ch. Flornell Sound Laddie.

The passing of the Edgerstoune Kennels was a great loss to the breed, since its fine stud dogs made available to the fancy the best of domestic and imported bloodlines.

The second of the pair began operations in about 1932 at Millbrook, New York when Miss Jean Flagler started her Relgalf establishment. Early operation was limited to Scottish Terriers, with Russell Openshaw as the manager and handler of the string. One of the initial purchases was a dog from England, Ch. Radical of Rookes, first champion for the kennel, which with Revealed of Hillwood and the bitches Sylvia of Hillwood and Reality of Hillwood formed the nucleus of the operation. Homebreds came rapidly and Relgalf was on its way.

A few years later the establishment was moved to Rye, New York where an entirely new and enlarged kennel complex became a model with everything for the comfort and development of dogs. Welsh, Airedales and Fox Terriers were added and the kennel population grew to around 60 dogs. Miss Flagler, then Mrs. Matthews, added Frank Ortalani to her staff, and the kennel soon provided stiff competition with a host of homebreds as well as its many fine imports, which now included such dogs as Ch. Flornell Soundfella, Ch. Flornell Sound Laddie, Ch. Silvertip of Gedling, Ch. Flornell Splendid and the great show bitches Ch. Rosehall Ideal, Ch. Broxton Battle, Ch. Ortley Angela, Ch. Cedar Pond Chloe (the last two from the now defunct Braw Bricht Kennels) and Ch. Grayling of Rookes.

The kennel had great success during the years 1940-1942 with two dogs: Ch. Bradthorn Bullion and Ch. Relgalf Ribbon Raider, a homebred. Between them they captured some 11 best in shows and were tops in the breed for the three-year period. Concurrently, Relgalf showed such Scots as Ch. Gillsie Dictator, Ch. Relgalf Rebel Leader and Ch. Relgalf Dictator to name a few.

During most of its activity, the kennel showed throughout the United States. It was not unusual to find Openshaw with his string in California or in the Southern States, and the name became a symbol of quality in the breed. While this mobility is not unusual today, with air travel at hand, it was quite an innovation at the time and did much to popularize the breed.

The kennels were closed shortly after the war; the 1949 season was

127

A gathering of friends of the breed at the STCA's annual banquet in New York, February 11, 1948.

the last for this extremely successful establishment. Relgalf dogs are still found in many pedigrees and their contributions cannot be stressed too highly.

One other strong establishment begun during the golden era of the thirties warrants mention before we leave this fabulous decade: the Marlu Farm Kennels of Mr. and Mrs. Maurice Pollak at Long Branch, New Jersey. The dogs were handled by Bob Braithwaite and later by Johnny Murphy, and both had great success with the string. In addition to Scotties, Marlu had a strong force of Welsh that were highly successful in the ring. Mr. Pollak bred many good ones, including such dogs as Ch. Marlu Crusader and Ch. Marlu Clincher, and he bought others. Eng. Ch. Walsing Warrant, an early purchase, was used well at stud while Chs. Deephaven Warspite and Deephaven Red Seal both graced the kennel pens during their heyday; their successes are history now. The closing of Marlu Farm Kennels was a real loss to the fancy.

This brings the review of modern dogs to the period of World War II. While activities continued on an abbreviated scale in the United States during the conflict, many fanciers dropped out and others cut down, never to return. Some, as noted heretofore, continued with good success and a few are still active in a large way.

The period from about 1946 brought in a host of new names, many for the first time and others as a continued effort that proved more successful than before. The list is so long that it would be impossible to name all who deserve mention, so it will be limited to those who captured the larger plums and thus have enjoyed national prominence.

As mentioned, Stalters' Barberry Knowe and Snethen's Shieling establishments were still robust competition for the best. Added to these were a host of newer competitors whose accomplishments have been outstanding. Heading this list is Mrs. Blanche Reeg, owner of the Blanart Kennels. Her interest in dogs commenced in the early thirties, but not until she bred Ch. Blanart Barcarolle in 1947 did her fortunes begin to brighten. Actually, Barcarolle's great-grand-sire was Blanart Bomber, a son of the incomparable Ch. Bradthorn Bullion, which indicates Mrs. Reeg's extended interest.

Barcarolle was finished by Mrs. Reeg in 1949 and then retired from the ring to the breeding pen. She produced ten champion get

130

Ch. Marlu Milady's Beau.

Ch. Marlu Milday.

Ch. Blanart Bolero.

Mrs. Blanche Reeg with Ch. Blanart Bewitching.

and a host of other good Scots that have helped bring the breed along. To date, ten of her progeny have produced a total of 56 champions, and many of today's winners have Barcarolle blood in their veins. Two of her sons, Chs. Blanart Barrister and Blanart Bolero, are possibly best known since each has been a strong stud force. Her granddaughter, Ch. Blanart Bewitching, one of the all-time great show bitches, holds an enviable record of seven best in shows with 20 group firsts and 13 specialty bests in her limited show exposure. She twice won the group at Westminster and was best in show at the International, to pinpoint three of her greatest triumphs. Best of all, she was invariably shown and conditioned by her owner, a notable accomplishment. During the past thirty some years, Blanart has bred more than forty champions and has owned many more.

The kennel was first located at Wantagh, Long Island but was moved to Boyds, Maryland where it remained quite active for several years. Mrs. Reeg moved to New York State and activity lessened progressively. There can be small question that Blanart dogs were a tremendous threat for many years, a tribute to the knowledge and ability of its owner.

Todhill is another kennel that has done extremely well in the postwar era both with homebreds and imports. Owned by Mr. and Mrs. Robert Graham of Rome, New York, it gained additional fame as the home of the great Ch. Walsing Winning Trick of Edgerstoune from the closing of Edgerstoune in 1954 until his death in October 1960. Todhill has had other toppers, however; these have won well and were also important stud forces in the breed: Ch. Todhill Cinnamon Bear, sire of Ch. Gaidoune Great Bear and Ch. Gaidoune Grin and Bear It; Ch. Friendship Farm Diplomat, sire of Cinnamon Bear, Ch. Todhill's Honest John as well as four Gaidoune champions in a single litter out of Ch. Gaidoune Gorgeous Hussy; and Ch. Special Edition, sire of a host of great ones including the show winning bitch Ch. Scotvale Sunshine, Ch. Wychworth Wizard, etc., among others. In all, Cinnamon Bear, Diplomat and Special Edition have sired some 37 titleholders, indicating the strength of the kennel's stud. In more recent years, activity has declined progressively as Mr. Graham has increased his judging activity while a move to Virginia reduced further the overall effort. Additional Todhill titleholders include Chs. Todhill Absolute Necessity, Todhill Fashion Mark, and Todhill's Oscar the King.

Ruth Johnson with Carmichael's Fanfare, best at the Scottish Terrier Club of America specialty, 1961, from the classes. Robert Graham, club president, left; and the author, judging.

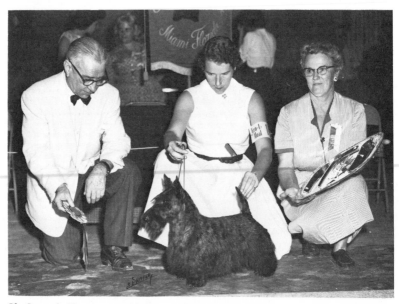

Ch. Scotvale Sherry, owned by Dr. and Mrs. Joseph Thomas, was BB at the Greater Miami STC under Charles C. Stalter, handler Ann Hone Rogers (now Mrs. James Edward Clark).

Among others who have been prominent in the breed but who have lessened or ceased active participation are Mr. and Mrs. Al Ayers whose Ayerscot Kennels bred many good ones. Active handling commitments over the past twenty years have made the Ayers curtail their own program. Mrs. Lynn Weaver (Scots Guard) is now an American Kennel Club field representative and so cannot participate in competition. Ruth Johnson of Carmichael's fame is now retired and residing in Florida.

Dr. and Mrs. Joseph Thomas' Highlander Scots included Ch. Wyrebury Worthwhile and Ch. Wychworth Heyday Hoagy, Mrs. Josten's Hampton Hill dogs with Ch. Walsing Wyndola of Hampton Hill, Cornelia Crissey whose Ch. Crisscot Carnival did so well and whose puppy bitch, Blanart Betwixt, won the 1965 fall national specialty of the S.T.C.A., the late Mrs. William Worcester, with a good winner in Ch. Gillsie Wrockwardine Sirius; Mrs. Louise Benham and Ch. Glendoune Gondolier and who still exhibits occasionally, Mrs. Sheldon Winans, whose Fulluvit Wee Mousie caused a sensation at Morris and Essex in 1951; Joseph Kelly whose great dog, Ch. Independent Ben, won the 1949 New York Specialty under the redoubtable William Singleton with Jimmy Murphy on the lead; Mrs. William Constable (Murray) who helped the wheaten but whose interest and activity in the breed was a never-ending source of amazement to all who knew her; the McLoughlins of Lynscot; Mr. and Mrs. Seth Malby (Rampart) and Charles Werber (Jepeca), Merritt Pope (Philabeg) and so many more that have done so much for the Scotsman. These are the people who kept interest alive after the war, while many are no longer active, most have a deep interest in the progress of the Scotsman and many are still seen at ringside.

Moving to more recent exhibitor-breeders who still support the breed at the shows we find that in the East, the Stonehedge establishment of Tom Natalini and Don Massaker is surely noteworthy. Small but select, a number of champions have come from its pens. One of the latest is Ch. Stonehedge Wildcat owned by Mr. Massaker and C. Kolb. Tom Natalini is a handler and this effort limits, to some extent, personal show activity. While the kennels are relatively small, they are quite successful. Ronald Schaeffer is another breeder-handler who operates on a relatively small scale but who has enjoyed

135

steady success because of sound breeding principles. He has bred such dogs as Chs. Schaeffer's Rocket Glow, Sky Rocket, his son, First Impression and Revelation among others. Mr. Schaeffer has a substantial background in the breed and at one time trimmed Scots at the Barberry Knowe Kennels, a useful credential and background.

Although relative newcomers to the breed, Mr. and Mrs. Bart Lapin have enjoyed steady success with dogs owned and/or bred by them. Ch. McRae's No Apologies was an early winner together with Ch. McLapin Just a Sample, shown by Judy Bonaiuto. Chs. McLapin Judith Kittle Bee, Jupiter King Bee and Brindle Brat are also typical products of the McLapin effort. In Connecticut, Mrs. Joan Eagle (Gren-Aery) has been gaining notice in recent years because of a steady run of titleholders including Ch. Gren-Aery Edward, sire of Chs. Gren-Aery Ferguson, McDuff and Tiffany of Pack Run, with more coming along each year.

One other eastern effort that cannot be overlooked is that of Mrs. Vana Mapplebeck on Long Island. Mrs. Mapplebeck's Ch. Lady Alberta's Scottish Ideal whelped a notable litter of five by Ch. Barberry Knowe Wildfire including, Lady Alberta's Ideal Citation, Wildfire, Annie Laurie, Scotch Piper and Ideal Creation. All completed their championship requirements before the age of three. Mrs. Mapplebeck has enjoyed showing her Scots with emphasis on multiple entry classes and has captured the award for best brace in show at Montgomery County (1966, 1967) and Westminster (1968). This unique effort recalls the fine competition for both brace and team laurels once an integral part of most large events, and always a spectacular sight since training multiple entries to show together properly requires both skill and patience. Of course, Mrs. Mapplebeck has had many other titleholders including the bitch that started it all, Ch. Lady Alberta (1960-1971). There are many more worthy fanciers in the Eastern United States, but to name them all would require a catalogue far to expansive. Suffice it to say the Scottie fancy in the Northeast is generously peopled with those that vigorously support the breed—a good sign for the future.

Passing to the West Coast, three fanciers that merit special mention are Mrs. Dorissa Barnes and the partnership of Martha Melekov and Lorraine Davis. Dorissa Barnes of Crescent Hill fame began breeding Scotties after the war with two English imports, Ch.

136

Lorayne and Bart Lapin with their homebreds Ch. MacLapin's Judith Kittle Bee and Ch. MacLapin's Jupiter King Bee, BOS and BB respectively at the Bald Eagle KC under breeder-judge Mrs. Heywood Hartley.

Vana Mapplebeck, an active supporter of the breed, has made a good record in brace competition. Here she pilots a well-matched pair to Best Brace in Show at Montgomery County 1966 under judge Percy Roberts.

Mrs. Dorissa Barnes with three of her champions, Crescent Hill Indian Scout, Crescent Hill Ace O'Spades, and Crescent Hill Maverick.

Ch. Marlorain Silver Spoon (Ch. Wychworth Windfall ex Ch. Marlorain Imogene), owned by Mr. and Mrs. I.E. Sprankle, She is shown here being presented with BB at the STC of California Specialty in 1963 by judge E.E. Vary. The handler was Daisy Austad and the trophy presenter was Miss Zsa Zsa Gabor.

Trevone Torquil and later Ch. Niddbanks His Nibbs. The first produced a bitch, Crescent Hill Ginger Blossom, which when bred to Ch. Wyrebury Wrangler produced the dog Ch. Crescent Hill Ace O'Spades, while the second sired a bitch, Ch. Milpita Mia Merriment. Ace O'Spades joined with Merriment to produce two of the kennel's best in Ch. Crescent Hill Maverick and later, Ch. Crescent Hill Indian Scout. In this author's opinion, "Scout" was a great Scotsman, and his record supports this contention. In all, Mrs. Barnes bred a score or more of titleholders and owned many more. Her kennels always placed quality over quantity and the results were most gratifying. Regrettably, Mrs. Barnes died in 1973 at which time the establishment was closed.

Marlorain started in 1952 with two half-sisters, Mariglen Blithe Spirit and Glenby Lorna. Both were by Ch. Glenby Captain, a son of Ch. Deephaven Jeffrey. Blithe Spirit completed her title and was bred to Ch. Deephaven Red Seal; the result, Ch. Marlorain Dark Seal, a great stud in his own right with some eight titleholders to his credit. In 1955 the kennels purchased Wychworth Windfall, an English import, and quickly finished him. He in turn produced three champion daughters including Ch. Marlorain Silver Spoon, which when mated to her grandsire, Ch. Marlorain Dark Seal, whelped a good winner, Ch. Marlorain Proud Piper. In more recent years, the kennel thrived with a host of successful show dogs including, Chs. Marlorain Rainmaker, Marlorain Dilemma of Burberry and Marlorain Alfie of Anstamm. Miss Melekov died in 1975 and the establishment is now believed closed, an unhappy ending to a well-conceived and productive operation.

Before leaving the West several others should be mentioned who have done well during the postwar period. Mrs. Edward Mansure of Merrie Oaks is one of these. Dr. and Mrs. Kenneth Grow and Ch. Garlu Haggis Baggis which under the tutelage of Daisy Austad did very well at the shows and attracted attention in New York in 1963, Mildred and Robert Charves who have had a number of good ones including, Chs. Charves Dazzler Dyke, Dashing DeJay, and Pacesetter among others; Mrs. Medora Messenger (Medrick) with Chs. Medrick's Monopoly and Medrick's Georgie Girl; Louise and Harvey Cederstrom (Cederbrae) with Ch. Cederbrae Witch Doctor; Gilbert and Neatha Robinson (Gilwyn) with Ch. Gilwyn MacKintosh and

Ch. Gosmore Gillson Highland King.

Ch. Viewpark Vanna.

the imports, Chs. Gaywyn Kilda and Gaywyn Guardsman; Mrs. Richard Swatsley (Revran) (co-owned with Mrs. Cederstrom) whose great bitch, Ch. Revran Reprise caused so much comment a few years ago (top bitch in the country in 1967 and 1968) and W.H. and Barbara Dunham's Castlecrag dogs are just a very few who have done much for the breed.

Before leaving the area, there is another kennel of considerable importance, to be mentioned. Mr. and Mrs. Clive Pillsbury (San Diego) added the Scotsman to their already-strong establishment in the sixties. Their Scots have since been prime contenders for top show honors many times through the efforts of several widely-known imports. Chief among these are Ch. Gosmore Gillson Highland King, a big winner on both sides of the Atlantic; Ch. Gosmore Eilburn Admaration, a dog that dominated the English shows in 1966 and '67 and who became an equally big winner in America; Ch. Viewpark Vanna who did extremely well together with Ch. Viewpark Vintner. The Pillsbury dogs have been conditioned and shown by Doug Bundock who has done an admirable job.

There are of course, a host of others on the West Coast who are dedicated to the breed, to mention all would be impossible. As in the East, the Scotsman is well represented and its many supporters are doing their best to maintain quality and breed characteristics. Lena Kardos, a veteran handler whose name is tied closely to the breed in California, is still a threat in the ring with a Scotsman. Over the years she has guided many to excellent records. One example is Roger and Nancy Abbott's Ch. Gaywyn Likely Lad, best of breed at the 1979 Westminster event.

In the South, activity has increased in recent years, possibly because of the proliferation of dog shows as caused by many extended circuits, so popular with professionals and amateurs alike.

The T. Allen Kirks of Roanoke, Virginia have a long-term interest in the Scot. They began about 1947, but did not have a first champion till 1957. Their first was a wheaten bitch, Ch. GranVue's Miss Manners. Once the ice was broken they began to achieve success rather rapidly with a long line of titleholders, some 30 to date. An import, Ch. Glendoune Gwenda, a great show bitch, was the starting point, along with Ch. Fran-Jean's Bridie Mollie. Thereafter, success was quite evident because of the sound bloodline set up by

141

Ch. Balachan Naughty Gal, owned by Mrs. Charles C. Stalter and bred by Dr. and Mrs. T. Allen Kirk, Jr., was a multiple BIS winner. She was piloted to her admirable tally by R. Stepen Shaw. They are shown here accepting the top prize at the Greenwich KC show under judge Stanley J. Halle.

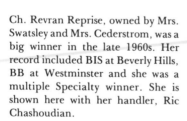

Ch. Revran Reprise, owned by Mrs. Swatsley and Mrs. Cederstrom, was a big winner in the late 1960s. Her record included BIS at Beverly Hills, BB at Westminster and she was a multiple Specialty winner. She is shown here with her handler, Ric Chashoudian.

these two fine bitches. In later years, Ch. Balachan Grenadier and the prolific stud, Ch. Balachan Agitator followed by such Viewpark imports as Chs. Red Hackle, a Bingo son, Dictator, Pilot, Truly Fair, Viewpark Viking of Cyann together with Chs. Balachan Night Hawk, Balachan Naughty Gal, a best in show winner and Neidfre Aftercummer were all standard-bearers for the kennels. Balachan has surely been one of the busiest of Southern establishments as well as one of the most successful. During the past few years, the Kirks have reduced their activities to concentrate on judging so that fewer Balachan dogs are seen in competition but the interest at this Roanoke-based effort is still extremely high. What is not appreciated by many fanciers who are new at the sport is that Dr. Kirk is a recognized authority on Scottish Terrier pedigrees, and his *Book of American Scottish Terrier Pedigrees* is a compilation that every person interested in the breed should own. It records the pedigrees of all champions from the start of competition until 1967.

The Heywood Hartleys of Florida and Virginia have contributed enormously to the sport and the breed. Both are now retired from active breeding and are most often seen judging around the country. The Hartleys bred their first champion, Woodhart Wendy, in the early forties to climax an effort that began years before. In all they bred and showed a dozen or more titleholders including a good brindle dog, Ch. Woodhart Wingover who represented some six generations of Woodhart effort as well as strong linebreeding to Ch. Edgerstoune Troubadour on both sides of his pedigree. Heywood Hartley had the honor and the pleasure of placing Ch. Carmichael's Fanfare at the head of the Terrier group at Westminster in 1965, the year she went on to best in show.

The Middlemount dogs bred by Bruce Webb are worthy of mention since he bred many fine ones in Florida, including about a dozen titleholders, among which were several wheatens. One of his big winners was Ch. Middlemount Juggernaut. Dr. and Mrs. Kater McInnes' Marymac prefix will also be found repeatedly in the records in view of their long-time interest. This leaves Dr. and Mrs. Stewart Carter of Louisville, whose Rebel Run establishment will long be remembered because of dogs owned and bred by them. Their first great dog, Ch. Edgerstoune Troubadour, bought from Edgerstoune, was purchased as a youngster of great promise and matured

143

to that promise. Troubadour became one of the top show dogs as well as one of the top studs of all times. He captured many best in show awards; the two remembered best were Chicago International (1952), with Jake Terhune handling, and Westchester (1954), with Johnny Murphy on the end of the lead. The Carters also bred the litter brothers Ch. Rebel Invader and Ch. Rebel Raider in addition to their full sister, Ch. Rebel Rhythm, all top show specimens.

Although Troubadour will always be remembered, the Carters are best known for their wonderful hospitality that made the Scottish Terrier Club of Kentucky's annual show one of the biggest and most popular in the country. Starting on a small scale, the Carters built it into a "must" specialty for any Scot to win in hope of national recognition. It brought the best Eastern and Western dogs into competition for top officials of the country to judge. The show was indeed a tribute to the Carters, wonderful people whom the breed could ill-afford to lose.

Other Southern establishments include the Camyscot kennels of Mrs. Elizabeth Myers and Mrs. Calvin Davis (Virginia Beach) that has owned and/or bred the likes of Chs. Camyscot Guid Giftie, Elizabeth, Sybbald (a Giftie son) and Cracker Jack. The dogs were often handled by Betty Munden, herself an enthusiast of the breed; Dorothy Morris of Maryland is another who achieved success and her Scots Delight line produced a number of good ones including Chs. Scots Delight Wild Oats and Scots Delight Rough Rider. Judith Bonaiuto, also of Maryland, whose Kirk Nor prefix is found on a host of titleholders, is another who began as a breeder and then, like Mrs. Morris, extended operations to handling as well. Kirk Nor has been responsible for many champions inluding Chs. Kirk Nor Outrider (BIS Winner), Sitting Pretty, Rubiyat, Ring Master and many more. Another Maryland establishment that is coming to the fore is the Kinsmon Kennel of E. and A. Watkins. Their good homebred, Ch. Kinsmon Noble Heir was among the leading winners in the breed in 1978. Three other efforts require notice because of steady success, the first is Stewart Gettle's Sagettes prefix which has done well even though limited to a relatively small operation. The dogs have won consistently and many pedigrees will show one or more Sagette dogs in the background. Two last Southern establishments are the Jaudon Kennels of R. and J. Barker in South Carolina that have bred and/or

Ch. Kirk Nor Outrider, owned and bred by Judy Bonaiuto, was a BIS and Specialty winner and is shown here winning the 1969 STCA Specialty in New York under Mrs. John Gilkey, Dorothy Morris handling.

Ch. Kinsmon's Noble Heir, owned and shown by E. and A. Watkins, was a consistent winner during the late 1970s.

owned a host of champions among which are to be found, Chs. Jaudon's Tomarhorn Honey, Jaudon's Highland Jester, Garscott's Jaudon Jezebel, and many more. Jester captured a best in show in 1974. The second of this pair is Miss Carolina Reid's Glenlivet establishment located in North Carolina. Of interest is the fact that Ch. Glenlivet Christina whelped a litter in 1976 that included five champions while Ch. Glenlivet Heatherbelle followed through with two titleholders in another litter the same year. The kennel's Ch. Glenlivet Gordon of Jaudon won a best in show in 1976 to add further glory. Gordon is a grandson of the aforementioned Heatherbelle.

As our survey goes westward, a kennel that has become a threat at shows all over the country during the past 30 years is the Anstamm establishment of Mr. and Mrs. Anthony Stamm of Kalamazoo, Michigan. In 1961, the Stamms imported Ch. Bardene Boy Blue from England and followed with several other Bardene Scots including Bardene Bobby Dazzler. These dogs established a strong, producing line that has been maintained successfuly through the years. Boy Blue won well from coast to coast with Lena Kardos on the lead while Bobby Dazzler had equal success. When Tony Stamm died in April, 1974, Mrs. Stamm continued the effort and even stepped up her exhibition and success. Such dogs as Chs. Anstamm Happy Sonata, Anstamm Happy Venture and a host of others have done extremely well and have been ranked with the breed leaders frequently. This is particularly true of Sonata who has captured many groups and best in show awards, while Happy Venture has become one of the breed's all-time top sires. Indeed, the establishment of a preferred bloodline which has been followed since its beginning has paid off handsomely with dozens of titleholders and should suggest to newcomers the great and lasting importance of intelligent planning. All of the great winning by the present group of Anstamm dogs has been done with "Buffy" Stamm on the lead indicating again that it does not take a professional to win if the amateur can do an equal job in the ring. Indeed, Anstamm is today, one of the most successful kennels in the breed and the major portion of this success goes to the good planning and excellent handling ability of its owner.

In the same general area, the Sandoone Kennels of Miss Betty Malinka (near Chicago) was one of the most successful during the sixties and seventies. One of the early products was a bitch, Ch.

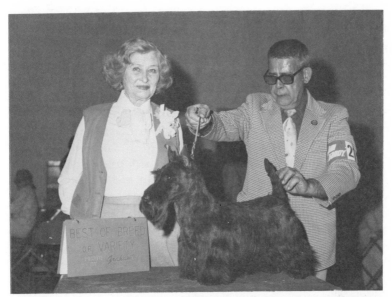

Ch. Glenlivet Gordon of Jaudon, owned by Carolina Reid, was a 1976 BIS winner. He is shown handled by A.D. Clay to a win under Mrs. Evelyn Tingle.

Ch. Anstamm Happy Sonata, owned, bred and handled by Miriam Stamm achieved great success in competition, amassing a record that included nine BIS wins.

147

Sandoone Missy Lou and since then a host of top Scots have come from its pens. It was a great loss to the fancy when Miss Malinka died in 1978 to close an era which she had helped so generously. One of her last big winners was Ch. Sandoone Royal Barclay (Ch. Sandoone Rob Roy of Milbran ex Ch. Sandoone Wee Wendy) who established quite a record in the middle seventies. Of course, Miss Malinka bred the great Ch. Dunbar's Democrat of Sandoone (Ch. Gosmore Gillson Highland King ex Sandoone Highland Heather), owned by Richard Hensel, who dominated the breed during 1976 and 1977 while continuing to do well in 1978. Bergit Coady, who was employed by Miss Malinka during her early years in America, handled both Barclay and Democrat to many of their triumphs. The loss of Miss Malinka will be felt for many years as she was a strong supporter of the Scottish Terrier and an intelligent breeder.

Expanding upon the activities of Richard Hensel's Dunbar Kennels, near Columbus, Ohio, one discovers another strong breeding establishment with numerous winners in addition to the aforementioned Democrat extending back into the early fifties. Some of the other successful dogs owned and/or bred by him include; Chs. Dunbar's Special Agent, Dunbar's Royal Flush, Dunbar's Deluxe Duchess, Dunbar's Downbeat, Dunbar's Abigail and the most recent headliner, the Democrat son, Ch. Democratic Victory. This dog is out of Ch. Prairyhill's Promenader and was bred by Mrs. Robert Willis. His career is just getting started as this book is being prepared, and he has already claimed best of breed at the 1980 Fall specialty of the Scottish Terrier Club of America under Mrs. Kirk and at the 1981 Westminster show under Melbourne Downing. Dick Hensel continues to breed and exhibit while increasing his judging roll and if past performance is any criteria, there will be many more winners from Dunbar in the years to come.

The Cantie effort of Mrs. Mary German began operations in Elkhart, Indiana many years ago and was later moved to Florida. It was most successful in the sixties and again, the dogs were handled by Lena Kardos. Chs. Cantie Captivator, Cantie's Ace and Cantie's Confident were but a few that did well. Mrs. German is presently more engaged with judging than breeding. Mrs. John Glikey was another successful breeder who began operations in Wisconsin and later moved to New Mexico. Ch. Gilkey's Johnny Come Lately was

Ch. Dunbar's Democrat of Sandoone (above), owned by Richard Hensel was one of the breed's chief standard-bearers during the late 1970s. The Democrat was fearlessly campaigned all across the USA by Bergit Coady. Ch. Democratic Victory (right), by the Democrat out of Ch. Prairyhill's Prom-enader, was bred and is owned by Mrs. B. Willis. At this writing his young record is already studded with a num-ber of highly coveted plums. He is shown with his handler Bergit Coady.

one of her better-known dogs while she was also highly successful with wheaten Scots and additional notice will be found in that section of this book.

Many other fanciers have had more than a modicum of success in the breed in the Midwest. For example: three Chicago area men who did their share to bring the breed along were P.K. Groves, Ernie Joresco and Bill Moore, known to many as Marie Stone's invaluable helper. Moving to Iowa, most will remember the Macauleys of Cedar Rapids, whose Mac's Welton dogs were known far and near. Also, the Misses Sanders and Portwood of Lansing, who owned the grand import, Ch. Glendoune Gaytime, shown as a veteran in 1965 at the age of 13 — she looked like a youngster, clear eyed and active; Math Rauen of Wisconsin, whose import Ch. Gillsie Roger Right and homebred Ch. Matscot Roger Ringleader have done so well on the circuits with Jack Funk. Allan Cartwright, Mr. and Mrs. Reason Krick, John Wright, Jr., and a host of other own successful midwestern establishments that produce fine Scottish Terriers.

At the present time, there is greater activity within the breed in the middle portion of the country than for many years past and during the last two decades or so, the number of fanciers has increased many fold and even with the attrition caused by death and loss of interest, the fancy seems to grow and remains in a most healthy condition. In addition to those establishments that have been discussed heretofore, a host of others require mention, some of long standing and others that have come into being more recently, these include, Dr. and Mrs. Barry Meador (Kansas) with Chs. Sandissy's Amazing Grace and Sandissy's Pettina Dee Lyn; John Sheehan (Minnesota) whose Firebrand dogs including Chs. Firebrand's Bookmaker, Firebrand's Foolish Fun and Scotsmuir Sandpiper have done well; Mr. and Mrs. Ed Fitzwilliam (Missouri) who have bred a number of winners bearing their name; John and Barbara DeSaye (Michigan) who have bred a number of winning Scots that they have exhibited both for themselves and for others including Chs. Sandreg's Keno Ticket, Candy Man, Editorial, Square Deal, Headliner and still others; Bengt and Cynthia Wallgren (Michigan) whose Terriwall Scots have provided strong competition including the likes of Chs. Terriwall Mischief Dazzler and Hinny Minny; Hilda and Ray Bigelow's (Ohio) Ch. Hil-Ray's Anchor Man, a big winner in 1971-72 together

Ch. Sandgreg's Headliner, owned by William MacInnes and Barbara DeSaye (handling), is a multiple group and Specialty winner and a successful sire.

Ch. Ruff Me Tuff Rabble Rouser, owned by Bill and Judy Shanholtz and bred by Jake and Nancy McCloskey, is a multiple BIS Winner and the top Scot for 1979. He is shown with his handler Landis J. Hirstein.

with a steady stream of above average, owner-handled dogs; Mrs. G. Catlin from the Chicago area who won so very well with Ch. Burberry Sir Lancelot under the guidance of Peter Green; the Kennan Glasers (Michigan) whose Kenjo dogs have been featured in the section directed at wheatens; Jake and Nancy McCloskey of Chicago who have had great success with their Ruff-Me-Tuff dogs including such as, Ruff-Me-Tuff Ready or Not, The Devil Himself, Rousta- of course, a Roustabout son, Ch. Ruff-Me-Tuff Rabble Rouser, bred by the McCloskeys and owned by William and Judy Schanholtz (Illinois). This was one of the top Scots in 1978, 1979 and into 1980 and was handled by Landis Hirstien. Many others bear mention because of long-time success in breeding and/or exhibition. These include Mrs. Goldie Seagraves (Ohio) a consistent breeder for many years, Helen Harbulak (West Virginia) who has exhibited a number of successful dogs including the winning Ch. Seagraves; Rogue's Image and Mr. and Mrs. Wilfred Schwer (Missouri) who had the honor of breeding, among others, Ch. Schwer's Dynamic Happy Boy. Owned by Jeanne M. Garlock of Colorado, Happy Boy was a strong winner and had BIS at Montgomery County in 1973 among his numerous laurels.

This brings us to a highly successful Ohio-based establishment that deserves some attention — the Wayridge effort of Mr. and Mrs. Wayne Ridgley, near Dayton. Originally called Ridge Lei, the name was subsequently changed to Wayridge. The fancy for Scottish Terriers goes back many years although Pekingese were bred and shown in the early fifties. In 1966, Ch. Ridge Lei Dazzler Dyke came along and finished in six shows while another Scot, Ridge Lei Dazzling Wendy produced four titleholders in two litters, both dogs were gifts from Mrs. Ridgley's sister, Agnes Page. Since that time, Wayridge has enjoyed steady success and has owned some 27 champions, 22 of which were homebreds. Ch. Wayridge Warlock has been a productive stud force with fourteen champion get to date. The Ridgleys maintain a small but select establishment where good bitches are the basis for their success, all reaching back to their foundation, Ridge Lei Dazzling Wendy.

Lastly, one of the strongest kennels in the land, as evidenced by its show and breeding record, is Gaidoune, begun in the fifties by Miss Helen Gaither of Wheeling, West Virginia. With Dr. Nancy Len-

Ch. Wayridge Warlock, owner-handled by Mrs. Wayne Ridgley to BB at the STC of Northern Ohio under Mrs. Edith Izant. Club President Richard Hensel presents the BB trophy.

Another Wayridge standard bearer is Ch. Wayridge Miss Page. This homebred was owner-handled to the title and is the dam of four champions.

festey as kennel manager, the effort has prospered and grown. It all began with the purchase of a bitch, Glendoune Gaibonnie from England. In fact, the kennel name, "Gaidoune" was coined from her name. Gaibonnie, finished her American title in 1956 and was bred to Ch. Rebel Raider, a Troubadour son. Out of the litter came the incomparable Ch. Gaidoune Gorgeous Hussy, a top producer in the breed. When Hussy was bred back to her grandsire, Ch. Edgerstoune Troubadour, the resulting litter included three champions. The following litter by Ch. Friendship Farm Diplomat brought forth four puppies all of which became titleholders. In 1960 she was bred to Ch. Todhill's Cinnamon Bear and produced four more champions including Ch. Gaidoune Great Bear, a top winner with 15 best in show awards and 47 group firsts. Her last litter in 1962 was a repeat to Cinnamon Bear and brought the kennels its second top winner, Ch. Gaidoune Grin and Bear It. Of course, of even more importance than his winning record, Great Bear's ability to produce was a major factor in Gaidoune's continuing success. Great Bear sired some 58 champions during his time with an amazing 60% of his offspring making the title.

In 1976, Miss Gaither brought Miss Barbara Z. Lundell into the operation as a partner. Otherwise, little has changed as the establishment enjoys continued success. In more recent years such Scots as Chs. Gaidoune Great One, Bear Garden (a best in show winner), Tinsel Glow, a good producing bitch, Gaidoune Lorilyn Bearcat (a best in show winner), Bear Bryant and Gaidoune Scotchow Sweet Bear are just a few from the continuing list of winners from the effort. The establishment has long since passed the century mark in titleholders, a satisfying accomplishment and a figure seldom reached by most. Of particular moment is the fact that Gaidoune is a breeder's kennel, very few purchases have been made as the homebred output has satisfied fully the demand for quality show and breeding stock. In 1979, the kennels moved to Stratham, New Hampshire and is now operating from that location.

This concludes the more detailed survey of specific breeders, owners, dogs and kennels together with some of their accomplishments. It is not in any sense complete and many worthy persons and equally worthy dogs have not been mentioned, a complete listing would have been impossible. Suffice it to say, that the breed has

Ch. Gaidoune Bear Garden, owned by Gaidoune Kennels and handled by Dr. Nancy Lenfesty, is shown going BIS at the Carolina KC show in 1967 under Mrs. S.J. Fishman.

Ch. Gaidoune Lorilyn Bearcat, owned by Gaidoune Kennels and handled by Nancy Lenfesty was yet another of this establishment's BIS Scots. She is shown winning the Terrier Group under Phil Marsh at the Conewango KC show.

Ch. Gaidoune Great One.

Ch. Gaidoune George W. Bear.

been fortunate in having had a host of supporters whose main objective has been to improve and perpetuate the Scottish Terrier and as long as it is blessed with such support, it will continue to flourish.

While numerous references have been made herein to Canadian dogs and fanciers, there are several that deserve special mention because of their accomplishments. Surely, one of the most unique efforts was offered by Mrs. H. Mellish in the fifties. She not only bred and exhibited Scottish breeds but trained them as well. Mrs. Mellish assembled a trained dog act, composed of six Scottish and eight West Highlanders, that performed frequently on the West Coast. The substantial success of this "Black and White" troupe negated completely the proposition that Scottish dogs are difficult to train. Mrs. Mellish had great success with her dogs in the world of entertainment and was a solid breeder as well.

Robert Sharp (Ottawa) also had substantial success using the suffix, of Seaglen. Most of his dogs had names with nautical connotations such as Amer. and Can. Ch. Rear Admiral of Seaglen and Supply Captain of Seaglen, while Amer. Ch. Glad-Mac's Wave of Seaglen and Glad-Mac's Sea Wren of Seaglen helped to perpetuate the suffix. Sharp gained his initial interest through Scots from Bernard Dittrich's Reimill kennels in England and these included Reimill Real Gem and Reimill Hydale Penelope. Subsequently Sharp's interest was more taken with judging than breeding. His death in 1976 was a real loss for the breed.

In the same general time frame, Fred Fraser (Ben Braggie) is prominent in the breed as well as maintaining an active interest in West Highland Whites. His expertise comes naturally as his father, Daniel Fraser, came from Scotland where he had a background of success with Scottish dogs. Thus, it is no surprise that the son does well with many Ben Braggie exhibits shown by himself and others all around both Canada and the United States.

This brings us to a prominent breeder-exhibitor who was well considered on both sides of the border. John Treleaven of Ontario bred and exhibited Scottish Terriers for many years and with consistent success. Further, he was instrumental in helping others gain a good start in the breed. Included among his many top dogs were Can. and Amer. Ch. Treleaven's Tobasco (grey-brindle) and an outstanding wheaten bitch, Ch. Yankee Pride Blushing Squaw, bred in

Heather Mellish and 14 members of her famous "Heatherbelle" Troupe. This highly trained entourage of Scottish and West Highland White Terriers appeared frequently on Canada's West Coast during the 1950s.

Ch. Gosmore Gillsie Scotch Lad, owned and handled by Fred Fraser, shown winning a Canadian BIS under the late Ted Joel.

Ch. Renaldo's Total Score with owner James Reynolds.

Ch. Renaldo The Muse, was WB at the Greater Baltimore Specialty enroute to her championship. She was owner-handled to this good win under the author.

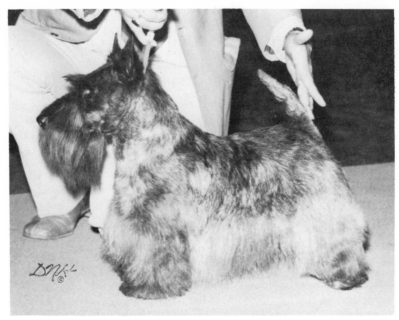

Ch. Renaldo the Rock.

Ch. Anstamm Happy Emigrant.

the United States by Peter Babisch. Few who were present will forget the stir she made at the 1962 national specialty show in New York, by placing winners and best of winners over a large, excellent entry, a stunning upset. Of further interest is the fact that James Reynolds, a currently successful Canadian breeder-exhibitor, credits Treleaven as being an early mentor, one who helped shape his initial course towards success. Reynolds' Renaldo establishment began operations around 1961 when he imported a dog from England. At the time, Reynolds was friendly with Treleaven who offered hints on trimming and also pointers on breeding. Treleaven suffered a stroke in 1964 and could no longer show dogs, and Reynolds was able to acquire a young dog, Treleaven's Top Brass from him. This proved to be a most fortunate acquisition as the dog did well in both the ring and the breeding pen. Top Brass was sired by Amer. Ch. Edgerstoune Troubadour and became Canada's leading winner in the breed in both 1964 and 1965. Better still, he was also a prepotent sire and all of Renaldo-bred Scots trace back to him, proving again the value of linebreeding.

Among the many homebreds that have done well for Reynolds are Renaldo Total Score, his daughter, Renaldo The Muse (a BIS winner) and Renaldo The Rock (another BIS winner), all are both American and Canadian titleholders. In addition, an acquisition, Ch. Anstamm's Happy Emigrant, has also become a big winner and an excellent stud force. Truly, Reynolds has enjoyed great success in the breed and continues his effort diligently while also pursuing a busy schedule of judging.

There are many other successful breeders and exhibitors above the border and the breed is in good hands with the Canadian efforts comparing favorably with United States trends where registrations are healthy, if not expanding, a condition that usually means improved quality over the years.

161

SKULL: long, medium width, slightly domed; hair short, hard

EYES wide apart; small, almond-shaped; dark brown or nearly black; bright; set well under brow

STOP slight

NOSE black, good size, should project somewhat over mouth

JAWS level, square; teeth even, scissors bite preferred, level allowed

MUZZLE in proportion to length of skull; not tapering too much toward nose

SHOULDERS sloping

CHEST broad, deep; well let-down between legs

FORELEGS short, good bone; straight or slightly bent

COAT short (about 2"), dense undercoat; outer, hard, wiry

SIZE: Height at shoulder, both sexes, approx. 10". Weight, males, 19 to 22 lbs; females, 18 to 21 lbs

BODY moderately short; powerful; well-ribbed-up, with strong loin; compact, well-muscled. Gait square, true; flexed hocks, stifles; forelegs incline slightly inward

EARS small, prick; set well up on skull; pointed, not cut; hair velvety, short

NECK moderately short, thick, muscular; strongly set on shoulders

TAIL never cut; approx. 7" long; carried in slight curve but not over back

HINDQUARTERS:Thighs muscular; good bone; flanks deep; bone heavy; hind legs short

STIFLE well-bent

HOCK to HEEL, straight

FEET round, thick; nails strong; forefeet larger than hind feet

COLOR: Steel or iron gray; brindled or grizzled; black, sandy or wheaten; white mark on chest objectionable but allowed

ELBOWS close to body turning neither in nor out

8

Interpretation
and Evaluation
of the Standard

THE Standard of Perfection for any breed is the specification set forth by breed proponents, generally the national specialty club that has been recognized and approved by the American Kennel Club. It prescribes the correct structure and temperament and is used as a guide by breeders and judges.

The standard is an important factor in the success of the breed. If it is sufficiently specific, it is relatively easy to understand; if it is too sketchy, it can confuse beginners and risk a wide variation of personal opinion among the more serious fanciers. Therefore a clear and concise standard is necessary if a breed is to progress. The Scottish Terrier Standard is an adequate specification. This chapter will examine its history and changes and attempt to clarify its more obscure points.

First it should be remembered that every breed was produced for a definite purpose. In order to carry out its purpose, its basic factors did not necessarily contribute to the dog's beauty but were necessary for his usefulness and sometimes his very existence. The Scottish Terrier was originally a working Terrier, bred to outlast vermin of all kinds and under all conditions. For this reason, the characteristics required for work should be considered of utmost importance when breeding or judging. First, temperament. The Scottie has to be fearless, not quarrelsome but unafraid of man or beast. He must be armed with strong teeth set in powerful jaws so that he can defend himself. He must own a good double coat, profuse with soft undercoat and well thatched with a tough and harsh outer jacket that will shed rain or snow and protect against briars, teeth and cold. He has to have a strong back and adquate hindquarters so necessary to any Terrier to aid in holding his prey to the ground; above all, he must have good, strong legs and feet carrying thick, tough pads, because the Scottie is an earth dog, a digger. Without this equipment, he is useless for his life's purpose. In addition, a Terrier of any breed needs sharp eyes, small and dark and well protected against injury beneath a strong overhanging brow.

These are the fundamentals considered of great importance; without them no Scottie could do the work for which he was bred. Many will counter, "Why worry? We do not use them for work anymore." This has some validity, but if we forget the basic background we will eventually lose the very characteristics that have made the breed great. For this reason, basic factors should still be guarded jealously by every person who loves the breed and who wants it to progress.

Interpretation of the standard varies with different people and leaves rather wide latitude for breeder and judge. The type of a breed can become modified through breeders' caprice and judging trends, which is why winning dogs from different eras look different even though they have all been bred and judged by the same standard. The detailed discussion offered here will aid the novice and will illustrate the latitude that may be taken with certain measurable points.

The first recognized standard of the "Hard-Haired Scotch Terrier" was written by Vero Shaw about 1882–83 and is quoted verbatim in Chapter 2. It was a rather clear specification subscribed to by most of the leading breeders and judges of the day. It left few points of controversy and helped the breed to progress after several years of bickering sparked by personal likes and dislikes. This early breed specification was adopted without change by the first-formed Scottish Terrier Club in America in 1895. It continued to be the law until 1900, when the reorganized Scottish Terrier Club of America, with J. Steele MacKenzie and Fayette Ewing as a committee, added a paragraph on disqualification. It read as follows:

Disqualification

Evidences of the use of a knife or other instrument to correct any defects. (The removal of dew claws being excepted.)

It should be the spirit and purpose of the judge in deciding the relative merits of two or more dogs to consider the approximation of nature to the standard rather than the effect of artificiality.

Thereafter the standard remained the same until 1925, when a committee of Henry Bixby, Robert Sedgwick, Henry T. Fleitmann, S. Edwin Megargee and Richard Cadwalader were called upon to revise it. The "new" standard differed from the original in many respects and eliminated the "half prick ears" that were previously permissible. It also changed the neck to include the word "moderately" before short; but the most important change was in the body. Where the early standard specified a "moderately *long* body", the new one called for a body that was "moderately *short*." Many other minor changes were included, and this standard reads as follows:

SCOTTISH TERRIER CLUB STANDARD

As accepted by the Club, February 12, 1925
and approved by the American Kennel Club

Skull (5 points): Long, of medium width, slightly domed and covered with short hair. It should not be quite flat as there should be a slight stop or drop between the eyes.

Muzzle (5 points): In proportion to the length of the skull, with not too much taper toward the nose. Nose should be black and of good size. The jaws should be perfectly level and the teeth square, although the nose projects somewhat over the mouth giving the impression that the upper jaw is longer than the lower.

Eyes (10 points): Small, prick, set well up on the skull, rather pointed but not cut. The hair on them should be short and velvety.

Neck (5 points): Moderately short, thick and muscular, strongly set on sloping shoulders, but not so short as to appear clumsy.

Chest (5 points): Broad and very deep, well let down between the forelegs.

165

Body (15 points): Moderately short and well ribbed up with strong loin, deep flanks and very muscular hindquarters.

Legs and Feet (10 points): Both fore and hind legs should be short and very heavy in bone in proportion to the size of the dog. Forelegs straight or slightly bent with elbows close to the body, as Scottish Terriers should not be out at the elbows. Stifles should be well bent and legs straight from hock to heel. Thighs very muscular. Feet round and thick with strong nails, forefeet larger than the hind feet.

Tail (2½ points): Never cut and about seven inches long, carried gaily with a slight curve but not over the back.

Coat (15) points): Rather short, about two inches, dense undercoat with outer coat intensely hard and wiry.

Size (10 points): About ten inches at the shoulder and weight about 18 or 20 pounds for both sexes. The correct size must take into consideration height fully as much as weight.

Color (2½ points): Steel or iron gray, brindled or grizzled, black, sandy, or wheaten. White markings are objectionable and can be allowed only on chest and that to a slight extent only.

General Appearance (10 points): The face should wear a keen, sharp and active expression. Both head and tail should be carried well up. The dog should look very compact, well muscled and powerful, giving the impression of immense power in a small size.

FAULTS

Eyes large, round or light colored. Light bone. Out at elbows. Ears round, drop, or too large. Coat soft, silky, or curly. Jaw over- or under-shot. Over- or under-size.

Further changes were made in 1932 and again in 1947 when it was believed that revisions were required to keep abreast of breeding and judging trends. For this purpose again a committee was selected which was composed of S. Edwin Megargee, Theodore Bennett, John Kemps, and Maurice Pollak. The standard they proposed was adopted and is still the one by which the breed is judged. The main differences between the '47 version and earlier specifications are an increased size which now reads: "19 to 22 pounds for dogs and 18 to 21 pounds for bitches," and the height for both sexes, which was set at about "10 inches" and was a far cry from the original 9 to 12 inches of the 1895 standard. The final important revision was inserted under "Penalties," where instructions were given to judges to turn down any dog for winners that does not have head and tail up. This last is a useful suggestion to improve showmanship and eliminate shy dogs, but it does not take into consideration the naturally dour temperament of the breed. Many judges who are not acquainted with the Scottie will turn down a better dog because the tail is not carried stiffly erect. This is not right for two reasons: first, the *Scotch Terrier*, as a basic breed from which all Scotch breeds were derived, did not carry a stiffly erect tail; rather, it was carried about three-quarters mast. Second, and more important, is the basic temperament of the Scottie. He is a dour dog that will not show if the urge is not there. This does not denote shyness, for which the requirement was incorporated, but rather a true Scotch temperament which refuses to do that which the dog does not want to do. It is believed that judges who know the breed can detect shyness in the dog's eye and that this should be the criterion rather than an inflexible turndown on showmanship.

A copy of the current Standard of Perfection for the breed is as follows:

Approved Standard of the
Scottish Terrier Club of America
Adopted 1947

Skull (5 points): Long, of medium width, slightly domed and covered with short hard hair. It should not be quite flat, as there should be a slight stop or drop between the eyes.

(1) *Muzzle* (5 points): In proportion to the length of skull, with not too much taper toward the nose. Nose should be black and of good size. The jaws should be level and square. The nose projects somewhat over the mouth, giving the impression that the upper jaw is longer than the lower. The teeth should be evenly placed, having a scissors or level bite, with the former being preferable.

Eyes (5 points): Set wide apart, small and of almond shape, not round. Color to be dark brown or nearly black. To be bright, piercing and set well under the brow.

Ears (10 points): Small, prick, set well up on the skull, rather pointed but not cut. The hair on them should be short and velvety.

Neck (5 points): Moderately short, thick and muscular, strongly set on sloping shoulders, but not so short as to appear clumsy.

Chest (5 points): Broad and very deep, well let down between the forelegs.

Body (15 points): Moderately short and well ribbed up with strong loin, deep flanks and very muscular hindquarters.

(2) *Legs and Feet* (10 points): Both fore and hind legs should be short and very heavy in bone in proportion to the size of the dog. Fore legs straight or slightly bent with elbows close to the body. Scottish Terriers should not be out at the elbows. Stifles should be well bent and legs straight from hock to heel. Thighs very muscular. Feet round and thick with strong nails, fore feet larger than the hind feet.

167

NOTE: The gait of the Scottish Terrier is peculiarly its own and is very characteristic of the breed. It is not the square trot or walk that is desirable in the long-legged breeds. The fore legs do not move in exact parallel planes — rather in reaching out incline slightly inward. This is due to the shortness of leg and width of chest. The action of the rear legs should be square and true and at the trot both the hocks and stifles should be flexed with a vigorous motion.

Tail (2½ points): Never cut and about seven inches long, carried with a slight curve but not over the back.

Coat (15 points): Rather short, about two inches, dense undercoat with outer coat intensely hard and wiry.

(3) *Size and Weight* (10 points): Equal consideration must be given to height, length of back and weight. Height at shoulder for either sex should be about 10". Generally, a well balanced Scottish Terrier dog of correct size should weigh from 19 to 22 lbs. and a bitch from 18 to 21 lbs. The principal objective must be symmetry and balance.

Color (2½ points): Steel or iron grey, brindle or grizzled, black, sandy or wheaten. White markings are objectionable and can be allowed only on the chest and that to a slight extent only.

General Appearance (10 points): The face should wear a keen sharp and active expression. Both head and tail should be carried well up. The dog should look very compact, well muscled and powerful, giving the impression of immense power in a small size.

(4) *Penalties:* Soft coat, round or very light eye, over to undershot jaw, obviously over or under size, shyness, timidity or failure to show with head and tail up are faults to be penalized. No judge should put to Winners or Best or Breed any Scottish Terrier not showing real Terrier character in the ring.

SCALE OF POINTS

Skull	5	Neck	5	Tail	2½
Muzzle	5	Chest	5	Coat	15
Eyes	5	Body	15	Color	2½
Ears	10	Legs and Feet	10	Appearance	10

Total .... 100 Pts.

Before leaving the written word of the standard it will be of interest to review the one presently used by the Scottish Terrier Club of England (1965). This differs in several respects from the American specification and suggests among other things, larger dogs having a shoulder height of 11 inches as a top limit together with heavier animals to go with the height. A copy of this standard is offered herewith to acquaint American fanciers with the English requirements:

General Appearance—A Scottish Terrier is a sturdy thick-set dog of a size to get to ground, placed on short legs, alert in carriage, and suggestive of great power and activity in small compass. The head gives the impression of being long for a dog of its size. The body is covered with a close-lying broken, rough-textured coat, and with keen intelligent eyes and sharp prick ears the dog looks willing to go anywhere and do anything. In spite of its short legs, the construction of the dog enables it to be very agile and active. The whole movement of the dog is smooth, easy and straightforward with free action at shoulder, stifle and hock.

Head and Skull—Without being out of proportion to the size of the dog it should be long, the length of skull enabling it to be fairly wide and yet retain a narrow appearance. The skull is nearly flat and the cheek bones do not protrude. There is a slight, but distinct drop between skull and foreface just in front of the eye. The nose is large, and in profile the line from the nose towards the chin appears to slope backwards.

Eyes—Should be almond-shaped, dark brown, fairly wide apart and set deeply under the eyebrows.

Ears—Neat, of fine texture, pointed and erect.

Mouth—Teeth large, the upper incisors closely overlapping the lower.

Neck—Muscular, of moderate length.

Forequarters—The head is carried on a muscular neck of moderate length showing quality, set into a long sloping shoulder, the brisket well in front of the forelegs, which are straight, well boned to straight pasterns. The chest fairly broad and hung between the forelegs, which must not be out at elbows nor placed under the body.

Body—The body has well-rounded ribs, which flatten to a deep chest and are carried well back. The back is proportionately short and very muscular. In general, the top line of the body should be straight; the loin muscular and deep, thus powerfully coupling the ribs to the hindquarters.

Hindquarters—Remarkably powerful for the size of the dog. Big and wide buttocks. Thighs deep and muscular, well bent at stifle. Hocks strong and well bent and neither turned inwards nor outwards.

Feet—Of good size and well-padded, toes well arched and closeknit.

Tail—Of moderate length to give a general balance to the dog, thick at the root and tapering towards the tip, is set on with an upright carriage or with a slight bend.

Coat—The dog has two coats, the undercoat short, dense and soft; the outer-coat harsh, dense and wiry; the two making a weather-resisting covering to the dog.

Colour—Black, wheaten, or brindle of any colour.

Weight and size—The ideally-made dog in hard show condition could weigh from 19 lbs. to 23 lbs.

Height at shoulder 10 to 11 inches.

A discussion of the several requirements in the present standard of the Scottish Terrier Club of America will be useful in its interpretation and to aid in evaluating the various points. The over-all appearance of any dog is of major importance. When judging a dog type, character and balance are important to consider. Any dog that lacks type, breed character and balance is not a good specimen even though his conformation is good, point by point. This is the reason that judging by the point system fails in many cases. Few standards give enough weight to type and character and overall balance (the Scottie standard is no exception), but stress various purely structural points. A dog may be perfect in each of these, but if the overall dog is not in balance, it is not a good specimen. Therefore, type, character, and balance should be considered, followed by specific structural factors. Holland Buckley said all of this in a few words when he remarked, "We must first strike for the true type of the breed, and bring our purely fancy points in afterwards."

Proceeding with a detailed discussion of the present standard we find that the skull should be long and of medium width, slightly domed and including a slight stop between the eyes where it joins the muzzle. In general, long-headed dogs prosper in the ring although today many Scotties are being shown that lack stop because emphasis has been placed upon extreme length. Lack of stop causes lack of brow or bone cover over the eyes and is a serious fault. Therefore, a stop should be present and when comparing two dogs of nearly identical quality, the one with stop and brow to go with it should prevail.

The muzzle of the Scot should be in proportion to the length of the skull. If the dog has a short skull, the muzzle should not be overly long since it unbalances the entire head. Actually, the skull and muzzle should be about equal in length, although it must be admitted that a muzzle *slightly* longer than the skull sets off the head and makes it more attractive, and dogs with this abnormality appear to be better in the ring.

The teeth of a Scotsman should be large and formidable. The upper incisors should meet squarely or slightly overlap the lower

Two typical Scottish Terrier heads. The head in this breed is very important to the total outlook and essential to the stamp of a quality Scot.

incisors, this being termed a level and a scissors bite, respectively. There should be six incisors between the canines (large tusk-like teeth) in *both* the upper and the lower set. This is important since some breeds are beginning to lose incisors and often only four are found. This is a fault that if permitted to continue will eventually lead to poor mouths. There is no leeway offered in the standard for "overshot" mouths, those where the lower incisors overlap the upper incisors.

The eyes, clearly described in the standard, should be relatively small, dark, almond-shaped and set wide apart. This means that the skull must be of *medium* width since a narrow skull will always cause the eyes to be set close together, which ruins the dog's expression. Round eyes are another bad fault, for here again, the outlook, foreign to the breed, offers a vapid expression rather than the keen, sharp expression that is characteristic. The paragraph suggests also that the eyes should be set well *under* the brow. This goes back to previous remarks concerning the presence of stop. The ears are described as "small," yet many of today's Scots have what may be termed *large* ears which detract from general appearance and expression. Mule ears, another common fault, are caused by the ears being set on the sides of the skull and not "well up" as required. Mule ears spoil expression.

The dog's neck is of great importance to the overall appearance of the animal. A long neck is always out of proportion while a short one offers a generally cloddy appearance. The standard, which calls for a "moderately short, thick and muscular" neck, is believed to be misleading since it does not describe what is wanted today. The English standard states the desideratum much better by calling for a neck "of moderate length." This is what is wanted, not a short neck. Proper length with well laid back shoulders offers a balanced appearance without being cloddy.

The body of the Scottie is relatively short in back and deep with well sprung ribs. The English standard elaborates on the rib structure by saying the ribs "flatten to a deep chest." This indicates that the Scot should not have a round rib cage but rather a heartshaped one with spring at the top and depth with a rather narrow structure adjacent the "keel." Many Scotties tend to be round-ribbed which

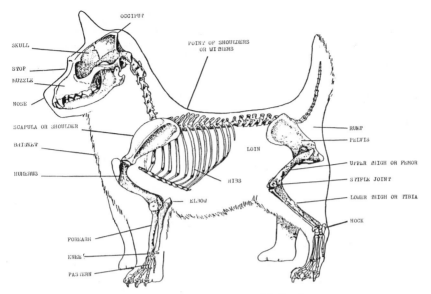

Skeletal structure of the Scottish Terrier.

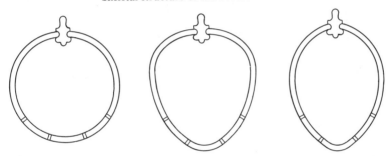

Rib structure. (Left) A round rib without depth, improper on a Scot. (Center) A heart-shaped rib, well sprung and with good depth. (Right) A poorly sprung rib not providing sufficient lung capacity.

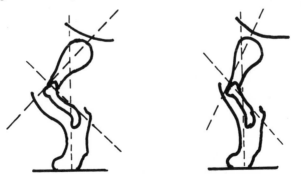

(Left) The shoulder with good layback provides overhang and blends the neck into the back to shorten the latter. (Right) The straighter or more upright shoulder lessens the degree of overhang and lengthens the back.

robs them of depth. In all cases, the elbows should not be below the bottom of the rib cage and this may be gauged by trying to place a finger or pencil across the elbows. If it cannot be done, the brisket or bottom of the rib cage is properly placed; if it can be done the body is shallow and probably quite round-ribbed. The chest, although taken separately in the standard, is certainly a portion of the body. It should be relatively broad whereby the front legs are set well apart. No Scotsman should ever have a narrow front of the order desired in the Fox Terrier. The brisket or "keel" should be well let down between the legs and should extend in front of the legs; in other words, the front legs should be set well under the dog. Too many Scots are being shown that have no "overhang," that is, the front legs are set forward and there is no body ahead of them. This generally indicates straight shoulders among other undesirable bone structures.

This brings us to the forelegs, which have already been placed properly with respect to the body of the dog. The legs may be relatively straight or bent with the elbows relatively close to the body. Short-legged Terriers never have as tight an elbow as the longer legged breeds since there is always some roominess between the elbow and the ribs. On the other hand, if the dog is "out at the elbow" this distance grows and is quite apparent upon moving the dog. The front feet are large in proportion to the dog since they were originally used for digging and for moving rocks and other impediments to the dog's progress in subterranean passages. The feet may point straight ahead; this generally indicates straight legs which are not natural so far as the basic structure of the dog is concerned. None of the early dogs of the breed had such legs since they would have been useless for the purpose for which they were bred. Dogs with slightly bent legs are more to the original type and these same animals have feet that turn out slightly. This is the proper structure.

Since the Scot is short-legged, it must, when digging, throw the dirt and debris sideways. This act is furthered by bent legs and turned-out feet. F. M. Ross commented upon this feature in her writings on the Cairn Terrier and stated: "No Cairn however deep or in what kind of soil he goes to ground, ever closes himself in. This may be attributed to the turned-out feet which help move the earth sideways instead of directly behind the digging dog. Cairns,

174

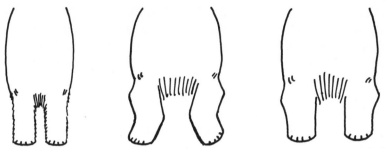

(Left) Narrow, pinched-in front suggesting a Fox Terrier build. (Center) Crooked forelegs out at elbows. (Right) Out at elbows.

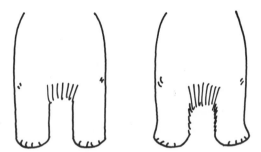

(Left) A good front with straight legs that seem to be acceptable to most judges. (Right) A proper front, the elbows close and the feet turning out slightly.

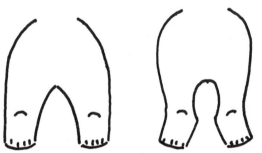

(Left) Proper hindquarters, the hocks turning neither in nor out, and spread apart to provide strength. (Right) Undesirable cow-hocks which, when turned in, tend to weaken the hindquarters.

Westies, *Scotties* that work should all have this type of foot, although accentuated turning out detracts from appearance and does not add materially to the working character of the dog." This passage is a sound evaluation of the reason for the condition and also limits the toeing-out to a degree that does not detract from overall appearance. The standard is silent on this point, which often causes uninformed people to fault dogs when they have turned out feet. The structure should only be faulted when the turn-out is excessive or when one foot is turned out more than the other.

The hind feet are smaller than the forefeet but are large in comparison with the dog. All feet should be well padded with thick, generous pads, and nothing approximating a thin pad or splayed foot can be tolerated. The breed is a digging breed and its feet are important.

The standard describes very well the characteristic Scottie gait. It is not like the gait of a Fox Terrier but rather a sort of roll, which causes a shift of the body so that the center of gravity remains over the vertical axis of the legs. This is required since the dog is shortlegged.

The hind legs are much as those of other breeds. They require strong hindquarters with well bent stifles and the legs should move in generally parallel planes, neither cow-hocked nor bow-legged. The movement should be free and easy with the front legs reaching out and the hind legs driving with a decided push. Some dogs will move with hind legs underneath them at all times; such a dog does not have drive, and when moving with one that does, will take two steps to the other's one to cover the same ground. Reach with driving movement indicates well-laid-back shoulders and properly angulated rear equipment. A dog that does not cover ground is generally poorly angulated in front or in rear, or both.

The Scot should have a thick, relatively short tail, not more than about seven inches and tapering from its base to a point at its extremity. Indeed, it should be carried stiffly erect, preferably with a slight bend towards the dog's head when he is at attention and never half-mast or between the hind legs. Early representations of the Scottish Terrier show the tail at less than the erect carriage and say that this is correct, but times have changed as has the standard.

(Left) Ears should not be large. (Center) Ears well set and relatively small. (Right) Mule ears, set on sides of the head, are very undesirable.

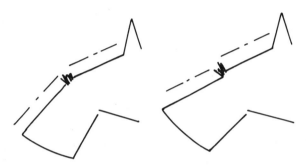

(Left) Muzzle and skull should be about equal in length from the stop. (Right) The top planes of the muzzle and skull should be parallel as shown by dot-dash lines, not down-faced as shown by the companion figure on the left.

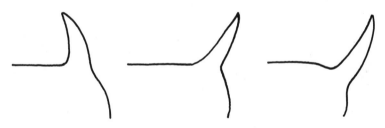

(Left) Proper tail well set-up and carried correctly. (Center) Tail correctly set but not well carried. (Right) Tail poorly set.

177

Today's Scotsman is required to have the proper shape, length and carriage of tail since nothing detracts more from the general appearance than,

"A gawkie tail, wi' upward curl."

The Scottie is a double-coated Terrier. This means that he should have a dense, soft undercoat and a hard, relatively long top coat. This should be about two inches in length when at its prime. The texture varies but should be as hard and wiry as possible. It will be found that blacks generally do not have as hard a texture as brindles, although there have been some that have owned exceptional coats. In all cases, coat texture can be improved by work but a poor coated dog can never be brought into a good coat. The color of the coat may vary through a wide range, including blacks, reds, grays, and wheatens together with brindle, and grizzle of any of these colors. Although there is no disqualification, white is not allowed and no more than a small patch or locket on the chest is tolerated. Dogs with excessive amounts of white should never be shown or bred, and although throw-backs of this nature may occur because of consanguinity with the West Highland White, they are rare today.

In general, the Scottish Terrier should offer the keen, sharp appearance of an alert dog. He should appear compact and strong, never weedy or light. The standard says he should present an appearance of immense power in a small size and this is an adequate description of the dog.

Before leaving the subject of the breed standard, I would like to comment upon the extent of modification thereof during the 86 years since the first specification was adopted in 1895. If one reads this early standard and then the 1947 version there can be little doubt that today's Scottish Terrier is a greatly changed dog from the early breed representatives. He has increased in weight from a range of 13 to 18 pounds to the present-day figures of 19 to 22 pounds; his ears must be pricked or upright, whereas he could have half-dropped ears in the beginning; his neck has been lengthened from "thick and muscular" to "moderately short, but not so short as to appear clumsy"; his body has been remade from one "of moderate length, not so long as a Skye's" to "moderately short"; and his height has been modified from the 9 to 12 inches at the withers to a flat 10 inches. Further, while it is not mentioned in the present standard, a dog should have a level topline, in differentiation to the statement in the first specification that he "should appear higher on the hind legs than on the fore." This structure was still apparent in the early 30's, as noted in the photographs of dogs of that era. These changes have possibly made the dog of today a more attractive animal but they have not added to his working abilities. Be that as it may, today the Scottie is a popular breed and one with a host of followers. One point that has never been changed and the one that draws so many to this breed is the temperament of the Scot. No other dog is like him.

Ch. Kinclaven Wild Oats, a classic wheaten Scottish Terrier.

Ch. Barberry Knowe Larkspur as a puppy.

Ch. Lady Alberta's Scottish Ideal, owned by Vanna Mapplebeck, and her puppies. Four of these ultimately finished their championships.

9

Raising, Training and Conditioning Show Stock

THE care, training and conditioning of good show stock require time and study. Show dogs do not "just grow" like Topsy; they are brought along carefully, and many a dog that would otherwise become an average specimen may be groomed and nurtured into a show prospect through intelligent care. I do not mean that a poorly conformed animal can be changed into a winner. I do mean, however, that many an average dog has done well in the ring through care and training, while many a good prospect has been ruined for exhibition purposes through lack of diligence in its rearing.

The average, well bred litter will include one or two youngsters worth working with for the first five or six months, when a more accurate estimate of their potentialities may be made. In choosing the most promising puppies in a litter, it is best to appraise coat, shortness of back and proportions of the head. The cutest puppies, those with the profuse and/or fuzzy coats, generally mature with soft coats requiring untold work to get into show shape, and then are on the poor side. Of course, if a puppy is otherwise outstanding, the balance may swing in his favor. A relatively short back, strong quarters, and well balanced head are necessities when choosing your future champion, so give these factors plenty of consideration before disposing of surplus puppies. It is a good idea to keep your first litter for at least six months in order to see how various points develop and retrogress. A little attention given the first litter will give you valuable experience that will pay off in subsequent litters.

It will aid in choosing promising puppies to watch the litter frequently at play at a sufficient distance so that your presence does not distract. In this way you can find our which puppy is the leader, the one that is "boss." Such an animal is generally an extrovert and will show well in the ring. You will also be able to observe tail carriage, ear set and general balance a great deal better than can be accomplished by having the puppies on a table where they are not at ease and are usually very tense. Added to these tests, find out which puppies like people the best, which ones come to strangers, and which keep their tails and ears up when being handled. When these characteristics have been determined, it will often be easier to decide which you want to keep. A well conformed dog that is not easily handled will be of little use in the ring. Of course, no irrevocable decision on the points should be made until after six months of age.

Feeding, first the dam and then the puppies, is important throughout the span of a dog's life, but of utmost importance during the formative stages. Feed plenty of animal protein food (meat) for substance, muscle and nerves, together with bone-building foods and a reasonable balance of carbohydrates, fats, etc. The diet should also contain calcium and vitamin supplements in the form of calcium salts, fish liver oils, preferably fortified, irradiated yeast, etc., although all supplements should be used with discretion since too much may be as harmful as too little.

The formation of strong bone and muscle is necessary if the dog is to develop properly. Weak, rickety puppies seldom grow properly, nor do their legs develop well. In fact, most weak puppies end up with bench legs, crooked and sorry looking. A poem found in Hugh Dalziel's book on *Discourses of the Dog* written in 1900 is apropos:

182

Ch. Raab Hill Merry Quite Contrary (above), owned and bred by Mr. and Mrs. Robert A. Marshall, was BB at the STCA 1966 Fall Specialty. The judge was A.N. Mac-Laren of Glasgow, Scotland, Mr. Marshall handling. Ch. Viewpark Red Hackle (right), a noteworthy winner during the mid 1960s was bred by Mr. MacLaren and owned by Dr. and Mrs. T. Allen Kirk, Jr. He was handled by Clifford Hallmark.

Ch. Ladysman, owned by Mr. and Mrs. Stuart Erwin, 1936.

Ch. Ardoch Souvenir, owned by John Deardorf, 1936.

There's some is born with their straight legs by natur,
And some is born with bow legs from the fu'st—
And some that should have growed a good deal straighter,
But they was badly nu'ssed.

The moral is clear—nurse them well, that is, feed properly and let nature take its course.

Exercise, too, is required by dogs of all ages. It can best be given to puppies in a good sized run either indoors or outdoors according to the weather. As soon as the youngsters can safely be taken outside they should be given the benefit of the sun's rays during hours of healthful play. If you can arrange an enclosed run, sheltered with plastic-coated wire netting such as sold for chicken houses, etc., you will be able to give your puppies the benefit of the sun without exposing them to the weather. Such material does not filter out the ultraviolet rays as does ordinary glass.

At about eight weeks of age, strip off all flying, fluffy top coat. This will permit normal growth of healthy hair which will develop into a good tight, straight coat, a great benefit to the dog in later life. Daily grooming from eight weeks on in the form of brushing will aid immeasurably in improving its texture and bloom.

While working initially on the coat, it is a good idea to remove the hair from the ears. This will lighten the ears and make it possible for them to stand erect. As a rule, a puppy's ear will rise normally to a half-prick position and then to fully erect. This may occur simultaneously with both ears or one may go up followed by the other a few days later. Once up, the ears may drop several times before standing permanently. In general, the ears should go up at from eight to 12 weeks of age.

Puppies should be wormed at about six weeks for ascarids (stomach or round worms), preferably with the advice of a veterinarian with respect to the vermifuge used and the dosage. If no worms are expelled, do not worm again for about four weeks; if worms are apparent repeat the treatment in a week's time. Two important admonitions: first, over-worming is the worst thing you can do to a puppy or dog, and may cause arrested development in young stock and a highly nervous condition in a dog of any age; second, never worm a sick dog or puppy. If the animal is not healthy and full of pep *do not* worm without a veterinarian's advice. After a puppy has reached four or five months, no worming should be done unless you actually see evidence in the stool and can identify the type of parasite. If you cannot identify the type, or see no worms, do not dose without consulting a veterinarian. He can make a microscopic examinination of the feces to determine the type of worms present and then prescribe the proper vermifuge and dosage, according to the dog's weight. A prominent veterinarian once said, "promiscuous worming has killed more dogs than the worms" and any experienced dog breeder will bear out this statement.

All puppies should be protected against distemper at an early age, first, by isolating them from any dogs that have been in contact with dogs outside the kennel, and second, by prophylaxsis and/or immunization administered by a competent veterinarian.

At approximately four months of age, the average puppy commences to lose his puppy teeth and acquire a permanent set. The teething period continues from one to two months according to the individual puppy. During this time, special attention should be given to the mouth. The puppy teeth do not always fall out. For this reason, if you see a permanent tooth crowding in alongside a puppy tooth, extract the offender and give the permanent tooth a chance to grow in straight. If you cannot remove the tooth yourself, enlist the aid of a veterinarian; milk teeth, however, usually come out easily since they have very little root. Many poor mouths can be attributed to failure to care for the teeth during teething, when in reality, the mouth was made poor by the owner's failure to aid nature. As a breed the Scottie has a good mouth, so keep watch over the teeth and there is little to cause further concern.

During the teething period, ears do funny things. Some ears will not stand erect before the puppy teethes, while others that have been up will drop. Personally, I prefer to help ears that are not erect at four months or which have dropped during teething. This may be done either by rolling them and taping them together at the desired distance, or by forming a tape backing for the ears and then taping them together. Either method is satisfactory. Another approach is to brush the ears with collodion. When it hardens, the film offers sufficient support to cause the ear to stand. In general, taping, etc., strengthens the weak ear cartilage and helps set the ears. Some ears may not stand for a long time and the taping must be repeated. The tape should be left on for a week or ten days and then removed before the ears become sore. Boric acid powder dusted around the base of the ears helps to prevent soreness.

At four to five months of age, the puppy is ready for preliminary show training. Lead breaking is the first step. This may be easily accomplished by first permitting the puppy to wear a light show collar for a day or two. The next step is to attach a lead to the collar and try gently to lead the dog. If he has a mind of his own, and most have, merely hold the lead and let the puppy balk and pull for about ten minutes. Repeat the lesson daily, for a few days, and you will notice that the dog's distrust of the lead lesens and that you can finally lead him around. In about a week's time, the puppy will permit leading for a walk. This should be short at first, as young dogs tire easily, then gradually increase in length until at eight months the puppy is walked about a mile a day in two periods.

This early lead training means much in later show experience. You will have a dog that does not fight the lead, moves easily and without fear, and is under complete control. Teach the pup to move on either a loose or a tight lead, at your left side, without pulling. Endeavor also to keep the ears and tail up by constant talking and periodic bribing with small pieces of liver or other choice tidbits. This makes the puppy a good showman—many an inferior dog has beaten a better specimen on showmanship alone! A good dog that does not make the best of himself is difficult to judge and a complete disappointment to his owner, while a good showman is always the "judge's friend."

Let the puppy run about the kennel or house while you are around and always keep tidbits in your pocket. Let the dog take a nibble occasionally, and before long you will have the youngster looking up at you even when being walked. This makes his exhibition a pleasure. During all walks with your puppy stop periodically and pose him as you would in the ring, make him stand with tail up and ears erect and with his neck well up. This gets him used to ring procedure and adds to his showmanship.

It is also useful to have someone not known to the puppy go over him now and then. This requires overall handling of the puppy and does not need any knowledge — anyone can do it. At the same time, have the lips lifted and gums and teeth examined. This will eliminate future antics when the judge wants to look at the teeth.

Lead breaking should be followed by walking your hopeful in congested areas where cars and people pass. This accustoms the puppy to the very atmosphere of a dog show with its excitement, noise and many strangers. A dog that does not shy at such things out-shows one that does.

It is also a good idea to train young dogs to ride in a car and in a crate for several weeks before starting to show them. In this manner, much of the excitement of their first few shows is eliminated as they ride like veterans and are comfortable and used to riding and crating. When first breaking a puppy to this experience, teach him to sleep in a crate by substituting it for his regular sleeping box. After a week of this, and when he is perfectly comfortable in the crate, take him for a short ride in it. Take him to the store or village several times for short rides. After a while he may be taken for longer rides until such time as he is perfectly broken to riding in a crate. By following this course of training, the puppy arrives at his first show fresh, not sick and scared, as would have been the case had he not been properly broken.

In the event he tends to be car-sick, you may administer a sedative prescribed by your veterinarian before you start out. This will calm his nerves and relieve car sickness to a marked degree. After several rides, you will probably not have to worry since most dogs are good travelers and like to ride.

The foregoing may seem like a great deal of trouble and work — and *it is* — but few, if any, dogs ever become top show animals without exhaustive training prior to reaching the ring. This is one of the reasons why professional handlers do so well. They spend time with their charges *before* they begin to show them.

Grooming your dog is the most important single item towards good show condition. This chapter will discuss general grooming techniques and requirements exclusive of show trimming, which will be expanded upon in the chapter to follow on "Trimming the Scottish Terrier." Grooming should begin at about two months of age and continue throughout the dog's life. Five to ten minutes'

Ch. Braeburn's Close Encounter, owned by W.R. MacInnes and Kathleen A. Conley and bred by R. and H. Girling. This bitch had a pair of BIS wins during 1980 and continued winning well as this book went to press. A daughter of Ch. Sandgreg's Headliner ex Ch. Anstamm Happy Moment, she is handled by George Ward.

Ch. Bardene Bobby Dazzler with Lena Kardos handling.

vigorous brushing every day will do more good for the texture and growth of the coat than any other treatment. It will also stimulate the skin and cause a flow of natural oils, thereby creating a healthy skin condition. At each grooming period, loose flying hairs should be plucked out and very little combing should be done, since this tends to remove too much undercoat.

In order to stimulate the growth of hair at selected points, warm olive oil massaged into the skin is good. This is especially helpful around the muzzle and on the legs as it softens hard furnishings and thus prevents the whisker and feather from breaking off. Rain water lightly brushed into the hair may aid in bringing out the bloom.

Anothe frequent task concerns nails. These should be cut back with nail clippers and then filed a little each day or two to keep them very short. This is especially true on the front feet, since the nails on the rear feet wear off more readily than those in front. Short nails improve a dog's feet and make them more compact, while long nails tend to splay the foot and break down the pasterns. This task should start at about eight weeks and continue throughout the dog's life.

Teeth should also be cleaned periodically, and this may be paced by the time required for a noticeable build-up of tartar on the teeth. Tartar appears on the canines and molars near the gum line and is the reason why it is necessary to remove it before the buildup becomes sufficient to cause a receding of the gums. Periodic brushing of the teeth with a regular tooth brush dipped in bicarbonate of soda and/or salt will do a great deal towards maintaining healthy gums and clean teeth. If the tartar does not come off it may be necessary to scrape or chip it off with a dental pick using great care not to injure the gums. In this operation, if you are not proficient, let your veterinarian do the work.

Ears and eyes should also be carefully watched. Bloodshot eyes may be eased with an ophthalmic ointment if the condition is caused by local irritation such as dirt, or by wind. If the eyes do not clear up within a day, the aid of a veterinarian should be enlisted promptly. Ears generally do not require any attention other than a periodic superficial cleaning, but they should be watched carefully so that canker does not gain a foothold. If the dog scratches his ears constantly or continually shakes his head, the ears may be in trouble. Examine them carefully and give prompt remedial treatment if indicated.

These are the major items of care. Early training, conditioning and general care will become a habit after you have raised a few litters. Knowledgeable dog people do the many things recommended in this chapter as a matter of course and if asked what to do, they would be hard pressed to tell you. In any event, following the suggestions here will help your puppy to grow into a better dog, physically and show-wise, and certainly will eliminate many of the difficulties that may arise.

Howard Snethen's best in show home bred, Ch. Shieling's Masterkey.

Mr. & Mrs. Henry D. Israel's Ch. Marlu Clincher.

191

Head study of Ch. Blanart Bewitching showing proper trimming of the head. Note that neither the whisker, eyebrows or tufts at the inner juncture of the ears are excessive.

10

How to Trim
the Scottish Terrier

THE art of trimming a Scottish Terrier or any other double coated, hard-haired Terrier involves ability and knowledge. It is not impossible to learn the art, but it will take time and more than the usual tenacity of purpose. Trimming makes a dog look smarter and improves its general appearance just as a hair cut or "hair do" improves the appearance of a man or woman. This operation takes a little time each day and the best trim may be decided upon by observation and comparison.

In all cases, a dog's trim should be personalized, that is, trim to make the dog look *his* best by bringing out good points and hiding faults as much as possible; never use a stereotyped pattern. One dog may require heavier trimming than another, one may require thinning of the coat, where another may need more coat. In other words, trimming must be carried out to suit the specified dog so as to present *that* dog in the best light, to accentuate good points and minimize the known faults. As Carlyle said:

The greatest of faults I should say,
is to be conscious of none.

Actually trimming is an art. There is no easy way to learn. Experience and knowledge are the only teachers. First, one must know how a good specimen of the breed should look, and second, he must be able to properly fault his dog.

This is why professional handlers often do better in the ring than the less experienced. The professional's dog is generally put down properly while the novice-trimmed animal is often poorly presented. This should not be a discouraging condition but rather a challenge to learn and do better. There can be no set formula since Scotties should be trimmed to suit the particular dog. That all good dogs of the breed bear a resemblance to one another is a tribute to the trimmer's art, since these same dogs, if stripped bare, would not look alike. Faults would appear that are entirely hidden by expert trimming. A good judge can find these faults. He not only knows what he is looking for but he knows the devious ways used to hide faults, and by use of his hands can quickly discover them. Often one finds a straight-stifled Scot, almost "Chow"-hocked, that appears to have good angulation. Upon inspection, it will be found that much hair is trained to stand away from the hock. At the same time, hair has been grown on the thigh to round out an otherwise weak hindquarter. The overall picture is good but the bone structure is just as bad as before the expert went to work. So it goes, faults are minimized, good points are accentuated until the dog appears at his best.

The trimming charts offered here are about all the help anyone can give; the rest comes with experience, appreciation of conformation and a knowledge of what is wanted in the breed. The fine points of trimming can only be mastered by hard work, mistakes, observation of experts at work, and experience, the same formula that is applied to every other breed that requires trimming.

Some learn slowly while others have a capacity to learn more quickly. Trimming of feet in itself is an art seldom mastered. Yet neat feet do more to set off a dog than any other single factor. Much the same is true of tails and ears. These are all-important in the trimming of our breed and the ability to trim these parts of the body

Ch. Special Edition winning BOB at Montgomery County, Pa., specialty, with Johnny Murphy handling.

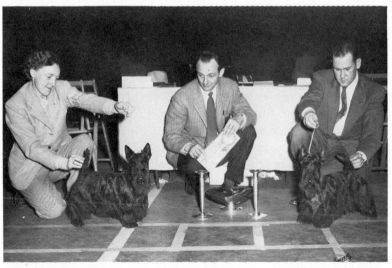

Winners at the STCA New York Specialty in 1955 were Barberry Knowe Wager (left) handled by Florence Prentice and Mar Eli's Make Mine Manhattan handled by Cliff Hallmark. The judge was F.J. "Bob" Bartos.

195

properly should be mastered first. The rest will come with experience, if you are patient and anxious to learn.

A good dog poorly presented has its chances of winning cut tremendously. This is not because the judge does not know faults of the dogs in competition, but rather because overall appearance generally has a strong bearing on the outcome of the placements. Type is of major importance and a dog poorly done often appears to lack type due to the faulty trim. On the other hand, a reasonably good dog properly put down exemplifies the proper type and even when hidden faults are found, it is difficult to beat him, for the most important act in judging is to pick dogs that look like Scotties. For this reason, faulty trimming often spoils the chances of an otherwise good dog.

This commentary on trimming does not answer the question of how a Scotsman should be trimmed because such a question cannot be answered by a general statement. However, any exhibitor who will pick up the challenge can learn through experience, study and intelligent observation. One comforting thought: you can never ruin a dog by trimming, for your mistakes will soon be obliterated by new growth of coat.

Tools used for trimming differ with different people but usually include combs, brushes and gloves, together with scissors, thinning scissors, clippers, and a stripping or plucking comb or knife. Scissors may be used for trimming around the ears and feet, although some adept individuals use the knife for all of these operations.

Thumb and forefinger plucking is nearly a lost art but the few experts who remain prove that it is still the best means for bringing along a coat. Using the plucking knife is the next best approach, since both methods eliminate dead hair while leaving live, strong hair in place, with the former being the more effective of the two. Clippers and thinning shears are probably the most often used for trimming; they are the poorest since they do not remove dead coat but cut it off along with the live coat, leaving the dead roots in the dog's skin. These tend to slow the growth of new hair and in some cases actually stop it, with the result that the dog's coat suffers badly. It is true that thinning a coat with thinning shears has its advantages but clipping has very little in its favor except speed. Yet clipping is generally used on heads and throats by most exhibitors both in America and in England.

The harmful part of clipping the body coat revolves around the double coat of the Scottie. Clipping cuts off all hair at the same length. This means that the undercoat as well as the harsh outer jacket is shortened. Since no hair is eliminated from its roots, the dog's coat is now shortened without proper conditioning. For this reason, if you do use clippers as a fast method of taking a dog down, be sure to grub out under coat and comb thoroughly before clipping, so that at least a portion of the dead hair is eliminated. After this, use the clippers.

Getting back to plucking by hand or with a comb or knife, take only a few hairs at a time. Grip the hair rather loosely and pull. Dead hair comes out readily and live hair draws through your fingers or finger according to the method used. This leaves the live hair in place, and it in turn can be shortened later, if desired, by means of a plucking knife held a bit tighter to cause some cutting of the live hair, or more appropriately, by singeing. This last seems to be a forgotten tool but it is very useful. A lighted barber's taper drawn across the dog's coat in the direction of the lie will singe off the unruly hairs and will also, if desired, burn or singe back the longer hairs to a more desirable length. Singeing should not be used until the coat is in condition as it is not a good means of trimming from the rough since, like clipping, it does not remove dead roots from the skin.

Many experts begin trimming a dog in the rough by the "spot" method. That is, they first remove the hair from the areas where it grows the slowest. A week or so later they take off another spot or spots and so on until at the end of about four weeks the entire dog is trimmed down, and the first trimmed areas are beginning to regrow. Thereafter, the coat is worked frequently, thinning and shortening where required and grooming all the time to keep the coat at its peak. Once the dog is in show coat, periodic work may be done to keep him in show coat. This is best accomplished by "rolling the coat," that is, taking off some of the coat, while leaving enough long hairs to maintain the coat's lying correctly. In time, three distinct coats will be carried by the dog, one coming, one prime and the other "going." When this is accomplished, the "going" coat is taken off at a time that another week's growth will cause the prime coat to pass over, bring the coming coat to prime, and permit new coat to "come." When this condition is attained, the dog may be kept "in coat" for months. True, there may be periods when the coat is not as good as at other times, but it will always be presentable and may be brought to its peak at any time with about two weeks' work.

The "spot" trimming technique may be all right for the expert but the novice is best served by overall trimming at the start. This means taking off all of the top coat and some of the undercoat on the body, head, neck and tail. Never completely remove the coat on the "drop" or "skirt" as it will require months to regrow. The same is true of the leg feather and whiskers. This hair is best brought along by selectively trimming the ends to bring the same to a more or less uniform length and by brushing the hair to keep it lively and to remove dead hair. All the while the trimmed body and head coat is being "worked" to maintain proper lengths at various parts of the dog. See the charts for more detailed information concerning the trimming pattern which, as explained, should be varied for individual dogs to bring out good points and minimize faults.

A good trimming bench or table is an invaluable aid when working on your dog and also helps to train him for show. The table should be of the proper height so that you may stand comfortably while working and should not be too large in area. A table about 25 inches long by 18 wide is adequate. Mounted on the side of the table near the front should be an adjustable upright from which can be suspended a slip collar adjustable to the proper height for each dog. This aids you in your work, keeps the dog's head up, and teaches him to stand properly. Instead of an adjustable upright you may hang a collar from the ceiling directly over the table. This collar may be adjusted for proper height from the table. Either method is satisfactory.

Actually trimming a Scottish Terrier will be greatly helped by following the diagrams in this chapter. Correct and incorrect trimming of various portions of the dog are here shown. Figure 1 shows a front view of a properly trimmed head with Figure 2 being a side view of the same. Note particularly that excessive whisker, eyebrows and ear tufts are not desired. The effects of such excesses are shown in Figures 3 and 4 while removing too much hair under the eyes and along the muzzle results in the grotesque appearance shown in Figure 4.

198

Diagrammatic Guide to Trimming the Scottish Terrier
Drawings by Mary E. Kornblum

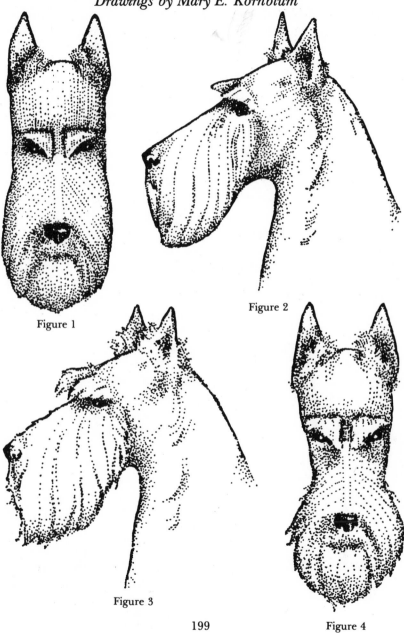

Figure 1

Figure 2

Figure 3

Figure 4

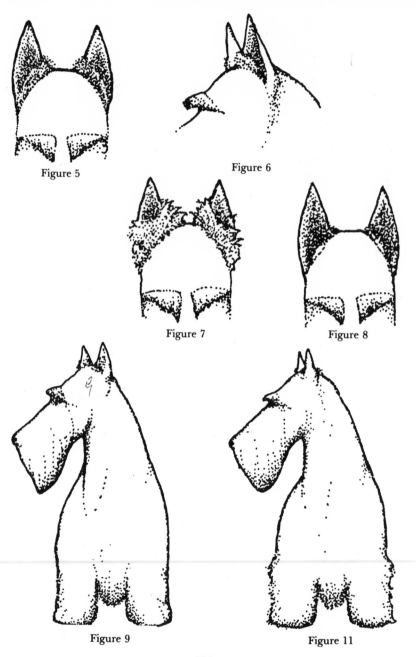

Figure 5

Figure 6

Figure 7

Figure 8

Figure 9

Figure 11

200

Figure 10

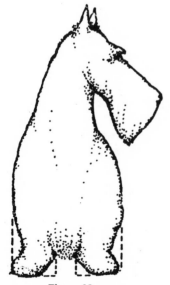

Figure 12

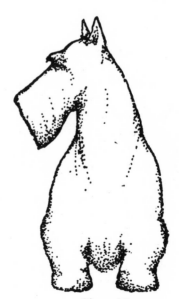

Figure 13

201

Proper ear trimming is shown in the front and side views in Figures 5 and 6 while Figures 7 and 8 illustrate the effect of too much and too little hair respectively adjacent the junction of ears, and head. In all instances, the amount of hair must be personalized for the specific dog being trimmed. A large-eared dog may require a bit more hair which makes the ears appear smaller. In other words, what may be right for one dog may be too much for another. This is why each dog must be carefully evaluated, faulted objectively and then trimmed to accentuate its good points and minimize its short comings as much as possible.

Figures 9 through 13 offer suggestions for trimming the front. Figure 9 shows a properly-trimmed front with even leg furnishings that blend smoothly into the shoulders. Figure 10 includes a side view of a well-trimmed front leg while Figure 11 shows a front with too much hair left on, particularly at the elbows and on the outside of the leg. Figure 12 offers suggestions for minimizing the effects of a poor front (fiddle front) wherein hair may be left within the dotted line areas to overcome the deficiency. A good judge will find this ploy but the overall appearance is certainly improved. Further, if the dog is not too bad in this area, proper trimming may eliminate the difficulty. Figure 13 shows the reverse fault to Figure 12. The dog in this view is out at the elbows and the front appears bowed. Here again, trimming may help and the feather at the elbows should be shortened as much as feasible, more hair cultivated on the outside of the leg adjacent the foot and additional feather carried between the legs. The net result, a straighter appearing leg. In all instances the feet should be trimmed neatly and appear well rounded.

The topline is probably the single most important portion of any dog and the trimming treatment is very important here (Figure 10, 15 and 16). In Figure 10 a proper topline is shown with a level, reasonably short back (from withers to tail set). The hair on the neck and blending into the shoulder may be left somewhat longer to suggest a better lay back and help shorten the back. Also, more hair on the front side of the tail may appear to improve back length. Many dogs have a distressing dip behind the withers as shown in Figure 15. In this case, hair must be cultivated and grown to help fill in this fault as indicated by the dotted lines in the diagram. It is not always

Figure 15

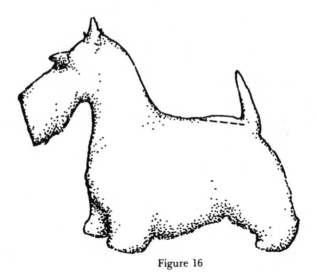

Figure 16

203

possible to overcome the fault completely but it can be lessened greatly by proper trimming. The same may be said for a "roached" back or a high stern. Here again, hair may be grown as noted in Figure 16 by dotted lines to help level out the topline while more hair grown adjacent the base of the tail will help if the stern is not already too high. A roached back or a high stern is difficult to disguise if it is very pronounced and in these instances it is best to forget showing the dog. In a few cases, a dog may develop a roach because of an anal abcess or related disorder. If the dog has always had a level back and suddenly develops a roach, this may be the trouble. Relief from the cause will generally straighten out the back without the aid of trimming subterfuges.

The treatment of hindquarters is an important step in proper trimming. This is a difficult area to trim and one that is frequently left till last and trimmed as an afterthought. Proper treatment of the quarters is shown in Figure 17 and in Figure 10. Note that the overall contour is trimmed smooth and full with the legs appearing straight. Figure 18 shows what will occur when too much coat is left adjacent the backbone. Here again, one must endeavor to present a smooth, well balanced picture to the judge. Figures 19 and 20 suggest ways for improving the appearance of cowhocks and bow legs respectively. In Fig 19, the cow hocked dog has hair filled in on the legs at both the inside and outside to make them appear reasonably straight. In Figure 20, the bowed legs are improved in appearance by growing more hair at the outside of the feet and filling in at the inside of the hocks. In all instances, the goal is to straighten the overall appearance of the leg and it may be accomplished quite well in many instances.

Figure 22 demonstrates what too much trimming will do to the appearance of the dog. Here, the hindquarters appear weak and lacking in angulation, all because of too much trimming. Also, the tail appears set on the very end of the spine. Figure 23 demonstrates the opposite mistake of leaving too much hair so the hindquarters lose contour and neatness. Because of the trailing "pants," the dog looks longer than it really is. This is why excess hair at either end of the dog should be avoided — it all contributes to the overall picture and sometimes alters that picture negatively.

The tail is the end of the dog and so is left till last here. Proper

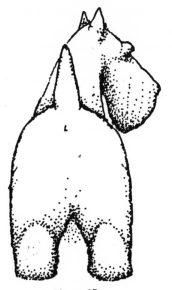

Figure 17

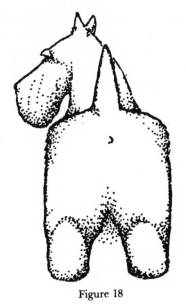

Figure 18

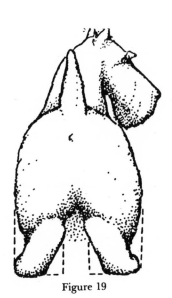

Figure 19

Figure 20

trimming of the tail is an art that many never seem to master. A tail should be made to appear both short and strong and the comparison to an "inverted carrot" is not amiss. The tail should be tapered and free from straggling hairs and it should be well covered with the major portion of its coat at the front side — much hair on the back side tends to lower the tail set. The tail coat should be well blended into the body coat as shown in Figure 10. The effect of too much hair on the backside is shown in Figure 25 and is never desirable. It seldom appears neat and, as stated before, tends to give the impression of a low tail set. Figure 26 shows a "rat tail" caused by over-trimming. This is neither attractive nor does it improve the dog's chances for winning. The tail here does not blend into the overall picture and such a trim causes the back to appear longer than it really is while giving the illusion of a poor set-on. Squirrel tails are sometimes seen on Scottish Terriers, and this condition is depicted in Figure 27. Again, proper trimming may be called upon to help the situation. A build-up of hair at the "head side" of the tail will help fill in the curvature and make the tail appear straighter than it really is. "Gay" or squirrely tails are not infrequent and while some fanciers attempt illegal surgery to eliminate the problem, trimming is the best recourse if the tail is not too curled.

These comments and drawings are about all that can be offered to the novice trimmer. They include basic advice and give a few thoughts on minimizing faults through proper trimming techniques. The first effort at trimming a Scot will never satisfy since the removal of hair is a simple matter but it cannot be replaced except by weeks of growing time. Thus, study your dog and your work and be critical as to where you have removed too much. Make mental notes and next time around you will be more aware and better able to overcome earlier errors. After a few trimming sessions, even the rankest novice can begin to turn out work that reflects steady improvement in ability. One point, in learning to trim be open minded. Ask more experienced exhibitors and it will not be too long before your trimming will reflect the expert advice. One comforting thought that should always be kept uppermost in your mind, mistakes will occur but they are always obliterated by time and the growth of hair. Be patient and learn from your mistakes. Trimming a Scottish Terrier is an art, and like any other art, expertise takes time to develop.

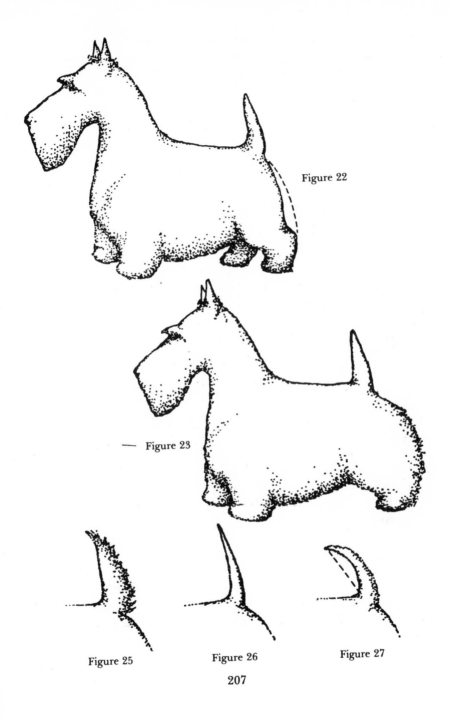

Figure 22

— Figure 23

Figure 25

Figure 26

Figure 27

207

When getting your dog ready for the ring it is best to wipe off the coat with a damp Turkish towel for cleaning purposes. The feather and whisker should also be cleaned or washed if need be. Thereafter, the coat should be thoroughly dried and, if it is overly long, towelled until show time. If the coat is the proper length or short, towelling is not required. Before entering the ring the dog should be thoroughly combed to remove all tangles and the coat rubbed over lightly with brilliantine or vaseline. This should be used sparingly and be well rubbed into the hands before application. The coat may again be combed and the dog is ready.

When the coat is overly long or when unruly hairs are present, a hair spray may be used — it is also useful on the feather and whisker. Lightly sprayed on, it will hold the coat in position. Some use "sugar-water" for holding the coat and in a few cases for stiffening the hair. This is a solution of sugar in water, boiled until dissolved. It may be of varying degrees of concentration according to the use. Rubbed onto the coat, it should be permitted to dry before combing. It will cause the individual hairs to adhere and in some cases, if not thoroughly combed out, will lend texture to the coat. Any judge who knows the breed can feel this and other coat stiffeners so the only benefit obtained is in holding the coat close.

An admonition on the use of sugar water that has a rather humorous twist concerns an exhibitor who was addicted to the stuff. He was in a rush to get into the ring one hot summer day and did not let the dog dry. The result was disastrous, since the dog was shown in a cloud of flies that enjoyed the sweetener and refused to leave the poor animal. Needless to say, the dog had a bad day — as did the exhibitor.

This is about all of the advice on trimming that can be offered. The rest is up to the exhibitor. Remember, however, you cannot help losing if your dog is inferior anatomically to another exhibit, but losing because of inferior condition or showmanship are conditions controlled by you and you alone.

Apropos is a remark accredited to the late George Steadman Thomas, well known Anglo-American Terrier expert, handler, and judge, who said, "The best looking dog will often beat a better dog put down indifferently," and truer words were never spoken.

11

Breeding Formulas, Rules and Axioms

WHENEVER a person becomes interested in breed-
ing dogs the usual question is, "What is the best way to begin?" Such
a query has a multitude of answers, many of which may be good
counsel. However, I believe the soundest advice that can be given
the tyro is to obtain a good, high quality, well bred bitch. With this
start years of heartaches and disappointments can be avoided. The
breeding of show dogs, show horses, and, in fact, any high quality
livestock is never easy. Persistence is generally rewarded and to those
who have tasted this reward, the work is worthy of the effort. To
quote a successful English breeder—"To attain continued success
needs patience and endurance and the optimistic temperament of
never ending hope."

Disappointment over the failure to breed a winner quickly has
caused many to drop out of the dog fancy. Thousands of fanciers
breed their stock every year with the idea of getting a show dog.
Many fall by the wayside when their efforts are not successful.

Most people begin seeking show honors in the wrong way and

thus delay their ultimate goal many years. There is no short-cut to high quality and, therefore, the use of inferior stock prolongs the time required to produce a winner. Of course, there are instances where a fine dog has come from parents of mediocre type, but these cases are indeed rare and such dogs seldom reproduce their own quality.

The surest and quickest way to be successful, which is attested to by all leading breeders of any kind of livestock, is to acquire the best matron obtainable, of high quality and unquestioned pedigree, and then line or inbreed her to the best stud dog available. Offspring from this mating may not be the ultimate, but the choice of the litter will generally be good foundation stock. No successful kennel has ever perpetuated the breed without an abundance of top quality bitches. Good stud dogs are many and available to all, but a good bitch is a rare asset whose value cannot be overestimated.

Thus, sound advice to anyone planning to begin breeding operations is to get a *good* bitch. This does not mean a puppy, but preferably a proven brood bitch, not over five years old, of successful bloodlines. Breed her well, and if only one litter is whelped she has done her part in the long-term program. From this litter, select the best one or two female puppies, if there is a choice, and breed them in the same family. The offspring of this second generation breeding will usually be of high quality and will stand a chance in the show ring if properly "put down," trained and shown.

Don't be "kennel blind." This affliction is defined as the inability, or lack of desire, to see faults in your own stock. No dog is perfect. Be critical, for to paraphrase Pope,

> Whoever thinks a faultless dog to see,
> Thinks what ne'er was, nor is, nor e'er shall be.

Look for and see the faults in your dog, for without knowing shortcomings, you can never overcome them by intelligent breeding. On the other hand, appreciate good points and use them objectively in the choice of young stock. Study the pedigree of your bitch and learn as much as possible about her forebears, their family good points and their family faults. With this information, you can breed away from these faults by proper selection of a stud dog.

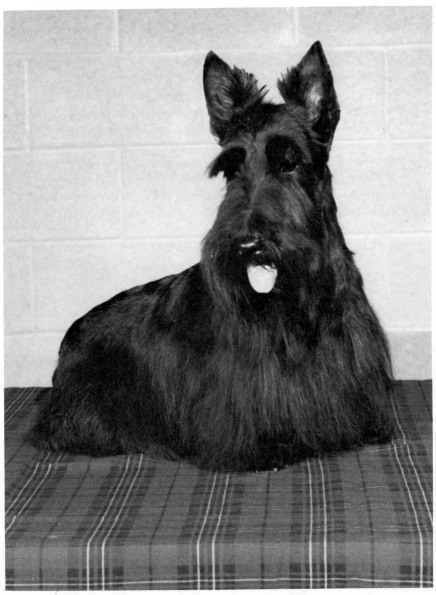

Ch. Glenlivet Heatherbelle, owned by Carolina Reid is recognized as one of the breed's outstanding modern brood matrons.

Family failings are of great importance; they generally overshadow individual faults. A dog from a family of poor-coated dogs, even though the coat is passable, will usually throw poor-coated dogs. Conversely, a poor-headed dog from a good-headed family will usually pass this fault to only a small minority of its offspring. Family faults are difficult to overcome, and intelligent breeding is the only means of rectifying the mistakes of previous breeders.

This does not mean that you should overemphasize families; at the same time, you should not overlook individual faults. For example, try to get for breeding purposes two individuals which do not exhibit family faults and are free from glaring individual faults. Endeavor to complement your breeding stock and try to use a stud that is strong in the weak points of the bitch, and vice versa. In this manner, you are combating faults from two or three different approaches. Never perpetuate a fault by breeding in a manner likely to strengthen that fault.

Character is all-important when selecting a stud dog. Bitchy dogs rarely produce well, nor do weedy, weak-boned dogs make good sires. A dog that is masculine, of good size and full of fire, with heavy bone and plenty of substance, has the best chance of passing on his good points. Such a dog is said to have "plenty to give."

Some stud dogs have the illusive quality of prepotency. Definition of this term is difficult; suffice it to say that it is the ability to reproduce good qualities. A prepotent stud, when used with the same bitches, will sire, on an average, more good puppies than an equally typey dog that does not possess this quality. Ch. Heather Necessity was certainly one of these as proved by his accomplishments. When choosing a stud, endeavor to find one that is prepotent as determined by his success as a sire. Champion dogs are not always the best studs; many fine dogs never enter the ring but produce as well or better than the popular studs of the day. Therefore, choose a dog that meets specific requirements, rather than the champion of the moment which may not be best for your bitch.

Age is another consideration. It is generally conceded that old bitches produce better when bred to young dogs, and vice versa. Animals within the range of two to five years old may be bred together but older animals are best bred to young, virile mates, while very young animals nick better with consorts of greater maturity.

Eng. Ch. Reanda Rutlin.

Eng. & Am. Ch. Westpark Derriford Baffie.

Howard Snethen's best in show homebred, Ch. Shieling's Masterkey.

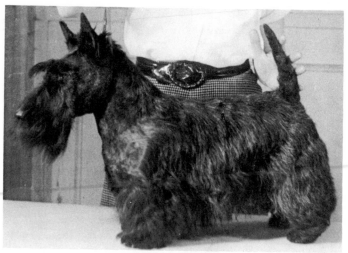

Engl. Ch. Reanda Rio Rita.

The bitch's type and character are important. Astute breeders say that a bitchy or feminine bitch is best, but no less an authority than A. G. Cowley (Albourne) allowed that a doggy bitch was the best producer. The argument could be enlarged upon but with little gain; so, to repeat, the bitch should be as good an individual as you can afford and can obtain. It is a fallacy to keep bitches for brood purposes that are not good enough to show. Wise breeders have long followed the course of using only the best. Somerville, more than 200 years ago, gave this counsel:

> Watch o'er the bitches with a cautious eye,
> And separate such as are going to be proud.

This is as good advice today as it was then, for seldom does a bitch amount to much that is not "proud" as exemplified by temperament, bearing and courage.

Certain breeding formulas yield the most satisfying results. Breeding in a line and inbreeding, as a rule, produce the quickest, best and surest results. Line breeding may be defined broadly as breeding within the same family. According to latest authorities, line breeding is concerned with the mating of two individuals, one of which is an ancestor of the other: for example, grandsire to grand-daughter. Inbreeding, on the other hand, is defined as the breeding of two related individuals, neither of which is an ancestor of the other and, generally, not over two generations removed, for example, half-brother to half-sister, first cousin to first cousin, etc. Both inbreeding and line breeding bring out recessive as well as dominant factors, and it is for this reason that family background is so important. Line breeding accentuates recessives to a lesser degree than inbreeding. Both types may be practiced with great success if careful selection of the mating material is maintained, together with careful choice of the progeny for subsequent breeding operations.

A third type of breeding formula is known as out breeding. This is concerned with the mating of two unrelated, or distantly related individuals. The latter is generally the case, although in Scotties there are several outcross breedings available due to the geographical sovereignty of the breed. Even here, it will be found that most modern Scots are related in the sixth or seventh generation. All of these formulas have produced well, with the first two being the most successful for obvious reasons.

There is one other type of breeding formula used more frequently than any other; this may be termed "random breeding" for want of a more appropriate term. Unfortunately, this path is followed by the majority and may be why there are so many poor specimens of every breed seen on the streets. This is directed to the practice of breeding a bitch to the dog that is available at the lowest cost in spite of faults, bloodlines or what have you. The results are nearly always the same: poor stock, generally poorer than either of the parents, which downgrades the breed with each successive generation. It has another unhappy result. When a bitch of this kind falls into the hands of a sincere person who wants to breed properly, it will generally require generations to straighten out past mistakes. This is the reason why any person starting as a breeder should buy as good and as well-bred a bitch as possible. It will cut years off the otherwise tedious road to success.

When practicing line and inbreeding the breeder should keep close check on the size and virility of the stock produced. It has been found that when too close breeding of this nature is carried on for several generations, a tendency sometimes develops towards loss of size and virility. These tendencies have been proved by experiments conducted with mice and rats. For example, Weisman and Von Guaiti inbred mice for 35 generations and found that the average per litter dropped from an initial 6.1 to a final 2.9. Ritzma Bos, when experimenting with rats, found that inbreeding was also responsible for loss in size. Average figures showed a 20 percent decrease in weight of offspring at the end of six years of breeding. Of course, dog breeders would not repeat these techniques for as extended periods as did the researchers, but the trend has been proved, and when the evidence is apparent, it is best to breed out of the line. This does not mean a complete outcross, even if one is available, but the use of a rather distant relative. The progeny of this mating may be bred back into the original line.

This word of caution is to allay the fears of many concerning the alleged "evils" of line and inbreeding. Selective breeding close up has always been the surest and quickest way to "set" good points. Since no moral issues prevail in nature, breeders should take advan-

216

Ch. Kinclaven Claudette.

Ch. Glennifer Tidbit, owned by Mrs. John G. Winant.

tage of these methods, while tempering their zeal with a constructive and critical eye on the results of their efforts.

The reasons behind the success of line and inbreeding may be explained by the theories expressed in the laws of heredity. Study of these theories will help explain many factors which are otherwise difficult to understand. Heredity is, however, a very intricate study. Many excellent books are available that delve deeply into the subject. For this reason, only a very short resume of the theories will be stated here.

The hereditary influence may be broadly surveyed by the application of the Law of Ancestral Influence. This law may best be defined as the diminishing influence of each successive generation of ancestors upon the inherited traits of a given dog. The parents are said to contribute 50 percent (25 each), the grandparents 25 percent (6¼ each), great-grandparents 12½ percent (1 $^9/_{16}$), and so on.

Arithmetically broken down as to the influence of each ancestor in pedigree form, we find the following chart to be illustrative:

Parents (50%)	Grandparents (25%)	Great Grandparents (12½%)
		G. G. Sire (1 $^9/_{16}$%)
	Grand Sire (6¼%)	
		G. G. Dam (1 $^9/_{16}$%)
Sire (25%)		
		G. G. Sire (1 $^9/_{16}$%)
	Grand Dam (6¼%)	
		G. G. Dam (1 $^9/_{16}$%)
		G. G. Sire (1 $^9/_{16}$%)
	Grand Sire (6¼%)	
		G. G. Dam (1 $^9/_{16}$%)
Dam (25%)		
		G. G. Sire (1 $^9/_{16}$%)
	Grand Dam (6¼%)	
		G. G. Dam (1 $^9/_{16}$%)

From this chart it will be seen that the more distant the ancestor, the less its influence on the dog. This also explains why line and inbreeding are useful. Either type of breeding reduces the number of individual relatives, increases their influence, and thereby cuts down the variables with which we must deal.

Eng. Ch. Westpark Rio Grande owned by Carnation
Farms.

Ch. Anstamm Dark Venture.

Mendelism is the specific application of the laws of heredity as applied to a given factor or factors. Dominant and recessive characteristics may be charted so that when breeding two individuals having known backgrounds, the results may be predetermined within limits. It is generally impossible to obtain the known background of many characteristics of a given dog, so that the application of the theory is sometimes difficult and often impossible to follow.

In color determination, however, it is very successful since the color of a dog is usually a known quantity and is noted on the registration certificate and thus may be traced back through generations of breeding. For this reason, the color of progeny from two individuals may be accurately foreseen.

Other breeding factors are not as easily predetermined by Mendelian formula due to unknown quantities in the backgrounds of the stock. The complexity of the problem is further increased by the fact that the same laws apply with equal force and effect to all characteristics. If an experimental breeding can be made, and if a breeder is patient and willing to sacrifice two or three breedings, he may predetermine certain factors which will be of benefit in future matings as well as in subsequent breeding operations. In general, however, the broad theory finds its greatest success in color determination. In this connection, breeders of the wheaten Scottie have found the rules most helpful.

Much of the foregoing advice is succinctly offered by a series of four axioms set forth by the late William McCandlish, author, judge and breeder of the Scottish Terrier. He proposed the following as rules to be followed to which I have added some explanatory remarks.

Like begets like — McCandlish says that this is more of a law than an axiom. The closer two animals are to one another in appearance and temperament, the greater the likelihood of the offspring being like the parents. Thus, if the parents are top specimens, the get should be good; if the parents are poor, the get may be poor or poorer.

Breed to breed — Meaning never breed with a mere litter in mind but, rather, with subsequent breedings from the offspring being of paramount consideration. Proceed with the view that the progeny will have improved breeding value over either of the parents.

Never breed from a second generation fault — Second generation faults are generally family faults that will continue to reproduce with increased emphasis. Conversely, second generation virtues indicate a dominant influence that is desirable.

No animal is well bred unless it is good in itself — The axiom points to the fallacy of breeding to pedigree alone. The majority of pedigreed animals are not show specimens, in fact only about one in ten is even a good specimen. The axiom stresses the necessity of using only animals with the best conformation and temperament for breeding purposes.

Deephaven Radiant at ten months old.

Phil Prentice with Ch. Barberry Knowe Kiltie in competition. Dog shows are more than a different diversion. They help identify the best dogs and influence the breeding trends of the future.

12

Value and Procedure of Dog Shows

W HAT is the value of a dog show? This question is frequently asked when discussing the advisability of entering a dog in one of these events. The answer is simple, and the reasons for showing stock are logical and sound. The only true measuring stick of breeding progress and success is comparison of the best you have with the best of other breeders. If your dog or dogs win consistently, you can rest assured that the type of dog you breed is desirable and that you are progressing in your breeding program.

Furthermore, showing of dogs keeps you on your toes. The results of the shows are a constant challenge to your ability. If your dogs do not win, or win very seldom, do not be "kennel blind" but begin to look for failings, and when you find them, start to breed away from these faults to improve your stock. Dog shows provide an opportunity for comparison, and there you may obtain unprejudiced criticism, such as a judge's placement of your dog with reference to other dogs. If, after attending three or four shows, you find that all the judges have similar reactions towards your entries, rest assured that their opinions, good or bad, are correct, and be guided accordingly.

Dog shows, with their long and varied history, are conducted differently in different countries. In England, the first event of bench type was held for sporting dogs at Newcastle-on-Tyne in 1859. sixty Pointers and Setters made up the entry. Judges for this historic affair included Messrs. J. Jobling, T. Robson, E. Foulger, R. Brailsford and J. H. Walsh ("Stonehenge"). Shows of varying success were held from that time until April, 1873, when the English Kennel Club was organized. It brought about a stabilization of the events and created their first real bid for prominence. S. E. Shirley, founder of the club, served as its first chairman and later as its first president.

In the United States, early history of shows is obscure, but honor for the first bench show here is credited to Hempstead, Long Island, near which place a show was held in 1874. Westminster was the first of the better organized clubs to hold a show and its initial event was staged May 7 to 11, 1877, in New York City, where it has been held continuously ever since. The following year, the Boston and Baltimore clubs held shows in addition to the New York fixture. The American Kennel Club was organized September 17, 1884, in Philadelphia, Pennsylvania.

Until that time, registration for dogs in the United States was with one of two early organizations: The National American Kennel Club, whose *Stud Book* was first published in St. Louis in 1879 with records for the year 1878, and The American Kennel Register which began in 1883 and was published by the magazine *Field and Stream*. The National American Kennel Club Stud Book was compiled by Dr. N. Rowe and issued additional volumes in 1885 and 1886, after which it was taken over by the American Kennel Club. These three volumes are now numbered one to three inclusive of the A. K. C. Stud Book. The American Kennel Register published five complete volumes plus two months into 1888 at which time it went out of business. In any event, we may take the 1884 date as the real start of organized interest in bench-type dogs and their breeding. The American Kennel Club did in the United States what the English Kennel Club did in Great Britain. It systematized dog show practices. Uniform rules were provided by an impartial governing body operating for the best interests of purebred dogs and their owners.

A class of Scottish Terriers waiting for the judge at the Wesminster show.

Ch. Glendoune Gwenda with Lena Kardos and Percy Roberts.

Dog shows in different countries, as staged by various kennel clubs, operate in different ways and award their championships after certain requirements have been met. English shows are divided into several classifications, depending on their importance and scope. The only shows that have any bearing on championships are those events termed, "championship shows." The remaining fixtures, which are numerically superior, may be likened to our sanction matches. The English championship shows are analogous to our licensed or member shows, in that a dog, by winning in its sex, is awarded a challenge certificate. No relation exists between the number of entries and the certificate awards; this is taken care of by the fact that relatively few championships shows are held each year (26 shows in 1979), thereby assuring a good entry with worthy competition. It requires three such certificate awards under three different judges to qualify for the title of champion.

In the United States, a different system prevails. To become a champion of record a dog must win 15 championship points (including two major shows) under three different judges. The number of points awarded at any given show depends on the number of dogs of the sex actually shown in the breed for a given geographical division. For example, in 1917, when the point rating system went into effect, the Scottish Terrier's rating was as follows:

Dogs and Bitches

1 Point	4
2 Points	7
3 Points	11
4 Points	15
5 Points	20

The breed enjoyed its highest point rating in 1939, when breed popularity was at its greatest. The rating at that time for either dogs or bitches was:

Dogs and Bitches

1 Point	6
2 Points	10
3 Points	15
4 Points	19
5 Points	25

Ch. Trevone Tartar of Bothkennar.

Ch. Hillcote Essential Knight, owned by Mrs. A.M. Henshaw.

Ch. Marlorain Proud Piper, Daisy Austed handling; Heywood Hartley, judge.

Ch. Cedar Pond Charmer, winner of best
of breed at Westminster, 1938.

The point rating for Scottish Terriers, as for all breeds, has changed many times in the ensuing years. Fluctuations up or down are largely dependent on show ring popularity and when major wins in any given division become too frequently encountered, the American Kennel Club will boost the number in competition required for winning major points.

Numbers and ratings will vary by geographical divisions of which there are four in the continental United States and one each for Alaska, Hawaii and Puerto Rico. The ratings are reviewed annually and published each year in the April issue of *Pure-Bred Dogs—American Kennel Gazette* as well as in the catalog of every AKC show. To determine the point rating for Scottish Terriers in a given division at a particular time, consult any applicable dog show catalog.

These changes emphasize the constant fluctuations in point ratings that are being made by the American Kennel Club in an effort to keep competition strong and allow for changing conditions in breed popularity. In this manner no dog can become a champion easily; he must meet competition consistent with the number of dogs being shown.

In general, the American Kennel Club endeavors to keep the number of three, four and five-point shows to about 20 percent of the total shows in a given division. This means that major shows (three-point or better) will be available but will not be so numerous that the average exhibitor can finish a dog in three shows. It also means that in a small registration breed, where competition is hard to find, it will not be impossible to finish a champion, which would be the case were all breeds to have the same rating.

Prior to 1917, the American system was entirely different. At that time the point rating at any show depended upon the total number of dogs exhibited at the show. Thus, it was actually possible for a dog to win five points without any competition. The ratings for shows were as follows: 1000 dogs and over, 5 points; 750 to 1000 dogs, 4 points; 500 to 750 dogs, 3 points; 250 to 500 dogs, 2 points; and 250 dogs and under, only one point. The obvious unfairness of this system revolved around the fact that at a one-point rated show, a winning dog might beat more dogs of the breed than at some other show where a five-point rating prevailed. The present system eliminates these inequities and permits the maximum point rating at any show, regardless of size, providing the required number of dogs in the sex of the breed are present.

Canadian championships are acquired in much the same manner as American championships except that only ten points are needed. The other requirements are substantially the same, and ratings vary in accordance with the numbers being shown in each breed.

The method of procedure and ultimate goal of a dog show is relatively simple to comprehend and is analogous to any other sporting contest where many opponents vie for honors. It is an elimination contest where dogs compete in relatively small groups and classes for the purpose of eliminating certain unsuccessful contestants. The winner of each elimination round progresses to the next higher competition for further elimination until only one dog remains, and that dog is awarded the title of best dog in show.

Every dog show consists of breed competitions usually subdivided by sex, with at least five regular classes being provided in each sex. These classes, together with their official definitions, may be found in Chapter 7, Sections 3 to 8 inclusive, of *Rules Applying to Registration and Dog Shows* (American Kennel Club), the context of which is briefly:

Puppy Class—for dogs six months of age and not exceeding 12 months. This class is open only to puppies whelped in the United States or Canada and entry must include date and place of birth, breeder's name and sire and dam.

Novice Class—for dogs six months of age and over that have not acquired championship points and have not won three first prizes in novice classes or a first prize in any regular class, puppy class wins excepted. Entry form must state place and date of birth, and name of breeder. Only dogs whelped in the United States or Canada are eligible.

Bred-by-Exhibitor Class—for AKC registered dogs six months of age or over (except champions) which are owned wholly or in part by the person or spouse of the person who was the breeder or one of the breeders. Dogs entered in this class must be handled in the ring by the breeder or by one of his immediate family. Entry must state name of breeder and sire and dam and place and date of birth of dog, together with the registered name and registration number.

230

Ch. Ashmoor's Roughing It, owned
by Bob (handling) and Louise Moore.

Ch. Deephaven Honeysuckle, shown with John Banks after her BIS win at the
Memphis KC.

American-bred Class — open to any dog six months of age or over (champions excepted) whelped in the United States by reason of mating which took place in the United States. Entry must state date and place of birth and name of breeder.

Open Class — open to any dog six months of age or over, except at specialty shows for American-bred dogs only, at which time the Open Class shall be for American-bred dogs only.

—Winners Class — open to the first-prize winners of each of the above five classes.

The above explanations are in their simplest form. Technicalities regarding calculation of age, eligibility to entry in the Novice and Bred-by-Exhibitor Classes, etc., will be found in detail in the definition of classes accompanying entry forms and also in the American Kennel Club booklet.

Entry may be made in any of these classes except the winners class, where entry is automatic upon qualification. All class entries, except in the Open Class, require careful study of the dog's eligibility. In general, young dogs over six months and under a year old that were whelped in the U.S. or Canada should be entered in the puppy classes for experience. After they pass one year of age, they are eligible for three wins in novice. They should then be sufficiently seasoned for entry in the upper classes. Before making an entry for any show, be sure to check the requirements of the class in which you are entering, since if the dog is ineligible your entry will be disqualified after the wins are checked by the AKC.

The championship points in each sex of each breed are contested for by the winners of the above mentioned five blue ribbon winners. These dogs compete in the winners class, and the ultimate winner is designated winners dog or winners bitch (purple ribbon), as the case may be. The two winners are the only dogs in the breed to receive championship points. A reserve winner (purple and white) is designated in each sex and may be any dog that has not been previously defeated except by the winner. The reserve winner is the recipient of the championship points in the event the winner is later disqualified.

Following the selection of reserve winners bitch, any dogs entered for best of breed competition, the winners dog and the winners bitch compete for best of breed. The best of breed class consists of cham-

232

pions of record, dogs which, according to their owners' records, have completed championship requirements but are not yet confirmed and the two point winners.

If one of the champions is chosen for best of breed, the judge will select either the winners dog or winners bitch for best of winners. If the winner here had fewer points in its own sex than the dog defeated, it picks up the higher rating. After best of winners is chosen a best of opposite sex to the best of breed dog is selected.

Should either winners dog or winners bitch take best of breed, it will automatically take best of winners. Furthermore, any champions of the same sex in competition would be considered in the point computation, possibly resulting in a higher rating. This also applies if the best of opposite sex goes to a class entry and it beats champions of its own sex to achieve the award.

Best of breed is designated by a purple and gold ribbon, best of winners gets a blue and white ribbon while best of opposite sex is awarded a red and white ribbon.

In the United States, champions are seldom entered in the classes in competition for the championship points even though they may be entered in the puppy class (if they meet the qualifications) or in the open class. This is not true in England, where champions are frequently entered in the open class for challenge certificate competition. Many arguments have been made pro and con, and it is apparent that if the practice were the same in the U.S. as it is in England, fewer champions would be made and possibly the urge to show dogs would be dulled among the less ardent exhibitors.

All-breed shows are further subdivided by the AKC into six variety groups which consist of arbitrary classifications of breeds that have some relation from point of use. Thus, Sporting dogs (Group 1) includes such breeds as Spaniels, Setters, Pointers, and Retrievers. Hounds (Group 2) includes Beagles, Greyhounds, Dachshunds, etc. Working dogs (Group 3) are represented by Doberman Pinschers, Great Danes, Boxers, Collies, etc. Terriers (Group 4) are all dogs that go to ground and include the Scottie. Toy dogs (Group 5) are self-explanatory, with Pekingese, Pomeranians, Chihuahuas, Toy Spaniels and Pugs being representative breeds. The sixth and final group is known as the Non-sporting group and includes a more heterogeneous collection of breeds than in any of the other five groups. Bulldogs, Boston Terriers, Dalmatians, Poodles, and Chow Chows are some of the members of this group.

The final judging at any all-breed show revolves around the variety group judging, and it is this phase in which the best of breed winner of every breed within each group competes for the honor of best in that group. In this manner, the show has been finally narrowed down to the six group winning contestants for the judge to go over for the best dog in show. The ultimate winner has eliminated every dog in the show to gain the coveted position.

Incidentally, if a class dog wins a group or best in show award, that dog becomes the recipient of the highest number of points available in the group or show, as the case may be. In this manner, if only one point is available in its breed and a dog ultimately wins a group or best in show including a five-point entry breed, that dog acquires five points instead of the original one. This applies only to dogs that have come up from the classes.

The foregoing is a brief explanation of show procedure. The same general plan is followed at specialty shows (shows for one breed only) except that group judging is eliminated.

Sanction matches are shows held for experience, and no championship points are awarded. These matches may be of the specialty or all-breed variety, for puppies only or for all-age dogs. They are a great deal of fun and excellent training ground for dogs and exhibitors, since they are conducted in substantially the same manner as point shows.

All-breed shows, specialty shows and sanction matches may be held indoor or outdoors and may be benched or unbenched. New rules make it mandatory for a club to state on its premium list (for point shows) whether or not the show is benched. If benched, it is required that the dogs remain on their benches throughout the show except when being exercised, readied or shown. This does not apply to puppies, which need not be benched until after they have been judged.

Premium lists are the prospectus of the show issued by each show-giving club. They list the approved judges and their assignments, show hours, and include prizes, entry forms, etc. Having exhibited at a show or two you will automatically be placed on the exhibitors mailing list and will receive subsequent lists for shows in your locality. If you are not on these lists, the show dates and superintendents' addresses are carried by all dog magazines and by the *American Kennel Gazette* months in advance. A letter to the proper official will bring a list promptly.

If you plan to exhibit dogs, endeavor to join a local dog club. Most cities have such organizations and they generally include a majority of the active exhibitors in the vicinity. Contact with these fanciers will help you over many rough spots and you can also learn through this association.

In general, dog shows are wonderful places to gain knowledge of your breed and of dogs in general. Professional handlers and experienced exhibitors should be watched as they prepare their dogs, and their actions in the ring should be noted. Most of them are willing to assist the novice if asked courteously when they are not rushed to show or prepare another dog. They were all novices at one time, since there is no means yet devised of skipping this phase. Intelligent observation and courteous questioning will help more than anything else to acquire the knack of showing dogs.

One more word on the subject of dog shows. While awesome the first time, they get under your skin. There is no more fascinating hobby than showing dogs. The bustle of the shows, the rush to get your dog ready and the thrill of winning cannot be equalled. To all this add lasting friendships built up through association with congenial companions met everywhere you exhibit, and you will appreciate why so many people follow the shows with interest, year after year.

Ch. Bothkennar Kilroy.

An enchanting tribute to the Scot's fidelity by Marguerite Kirmse.

13

Helpful Facts
and Figures

THIS chapter, more or less statistical in nature, will
offer the reader a collection of unrelated data and interesting facts
concerning the Scottish Terrier. It will give registration figures for
the breed in America for the 15-year period from 1966 through
1980. It will list the number of American champions of record by
years for the same period.

In addition, there is a tabulation of all Scottish Terriers that have
won best in show at any all-breed event in the United States during
the period, and in this manner many quality dogs not previously
mentioned will be given credit for their excellence.

As an added feature, a list of fanciers together with their kennel
names covers many of the more prominent breed devotees in America and Britain. The above facts will aid in rounding out a knowledge of the breed that may be helpful to tyros and useful to old-timers.

Registration Figures for Scottish Terriers
1966–1980 inclusive

Year	Individual Registrations		Championships Completed	Registrations per Champion
1966	6571	(23)	87	75.5
1967	7519	(24)	78	96.4
1968	8308	(24)	83	100.0
1969	9710	(24)	97	100.1
1970	10248	(25)	106	96.7
1971	10756	(24)	91	118.3
1972	10011	(28)	110	91.0
1973	9502	(30)	109	87.2
1974	8819	(32)	95	92.8
1975	7380	(34)	121	61.0
1976	7202	(34)	105	68.6
1977	7073	(34)	115	61.5
1978	6430	(35)	108	59.5
1979	6343	(36)	136	46.6
1980	6334	(36)	134	47.3

The above figures show the downward trend Scottish Terrier registrations have taken since 1972. Some will consider this a beneficial development, pointing to the fact that the decline would tend to discourage commercial interests. Others will interpret the figures to mean a general lessening of interest across the board, and this is surely not a good thing. It is the responsibility of the fancier to present the breed in its most favorable light. This can be accomplished by breeding selectively and retaining only the finest examples of what is produced. Only by the most ruthless selection will Scottish Terrier breeders be able to produce dogs of above average quality.

Best in Show Winning Scottish Terriers for the Years 1966–1980 (AKC All-Breed Shows only)

1966 Total — 13

Ch. Bardene Bingo*	11
Ch. Barberry Knowe Bingo	1
Ch Barberry Knowe Blizzard	1

1967 Total — 8

Ch. Bardene Bingo*	2
Ch. Gaidoune Bear Garden	2
Ch. Gaidoune Great One	2
Ch. Carnation Casino	1
Ch. Revran Reprise	1

Eng. & Am. Ch. Reimill Radiator.

Eng. Ch. Glenview Fancy Lad, owned by Maureen
Micklethwaite and Mr. A.H. Gee and bred by Mr. Gee.

1968 Total — 6
        Ch. Balachan Night Hawk   4
        Ch. Firebrand's Dark Velour   1
        Ch. Gosmore Gilson Highland King*   1

1969 Total — 6
        Ch. Gosmore Eilburn Admaration*   3
        Ch. Gaidoude Great Marshall Bear   1
        Ch. Rantin' Robin of Lakelynn*   1

1970 Total — 5
        Ch. Gosmore EIlburn Admaration*   2
        Camyscot Sybbald   1
        Ch. Gaidoune George W. Bear   1
        Ch. Kirk Nor Outrider   1

1971 Total — 8
        Ch. Balachan Naughty Gal   3
        Ch. Firebrand's Bookmaker   3
        Ch. Gaidoune George W. Bear   1
        Ch. Seagrave's Rogue's Image   1

1972 Total — 5
        Ch. Gaidoune George W. Bear   2
        Ch. Balachan Naughty Gal   1
        Ch. Firebrand's Bookmaker   1
        Ch. Gaidoune Lorilyn Bearcat   1

1973 Total — 4
        Ch. Schwer's Dynamic Happy Boy   2
        Ch. Balachan Naughty Gal   1
        Ch. Gaidoune Lorilyn Bearcat   1

1974 Total — 1
        Ch. Jaudon's Highland Jester   1

1975 Total — 4
        Ch. Bear-Bee's Bit of Dunbar   1
        Ch. Burbury's Sir Lancelot   1
        Ch. Dunbar's Distinction   1
        Ch. Gidoune Oh Hugh Bear   1

1976 Total — 7
        Ch. Dunbar's Democrat of Sandoone   4
        Ch. Sonata Serenade   2
        Ch. Glenlivet Gordon of Jaudon   1

1977 Total — 20
        Ch. Dunbar's Democrat of Sandoone   14
        Ch. Anstamm Happy Sonata   5
        Ch. Firebrand's Foolish Fun   1

Ch. Marlorain Dark Seal.

Eng. Ch. Glenecker Golden Girl, owned and bred by
Maureen Micklethwaite, was only the eighth wheaten
champion in the history of British dog shows.

Ch. Todhill's Cinnamon Bear, owned by Mr. and Mrs. R. C. Graham, was a strong winner and an important stud force in the breed. He is shown here with handler, John P. Murphy.

Ch. Glendoune Gondolier, owned by Louise Benham was the author's choice for BB at the 1959 Westminster show. This import was handled by Robert Gorman.

1978 Total — 7
        Ch. Anstamm Happy Sonata   4
        Ch. Clanronald's Watch My Smoke   1
        Ch. Firebrand's Foolish Fun   1
        Ch. Hughcrest Bottoms Up   1

1979 Total — 4
        Ch. Ruff Me Tuff Rabble Rouser   2
        Ch. Schaeffer's Calling Card   1
        Ch. Scot's Bairn's Gambler's Dream   1

1980 Total — 5
        Ch. Braeburn's Close Encounter   2
        Ch. Ruff Me Tuff Rabble Rouser   2
        Ch. Democratic Victory   1

* Indicates an import

The best in show record for Scottish Terriers, like registration figures, offers an interesting if considerably contrasting situation to the period 1956 through 1965. During the past 15 years the breed totaled 103 bests in show compared to the 139 of the earlier period. These wins were made by 39 dogs compared to the 41 who turned the trick as shown in the last edition of this book. The dramatic shift concerns the place of the import among top winners. Only four of the more recent best in show dogs were British imports and this quartet accounted for twenty of the top wins made by Scots.

Making a Champion—American and English Systems

While the numbers of British champions for the period 1966-1980 are not offered here, it is very safe to say that there are always many more American title holders than British ones. The reasons for this are the systems in operation for dog shows here and in the British Isles. In America championship points are available at some 600 to 800 shows held all over the country. In Britain challenge certificates counting toward a championship are only offered at some two dozen events in any given year. This limited opportunity, combined with the fact that in Britain champions are always shown in the open class, serves to keep competition keen and the quality of the British champion high.

Kennel Names and Their Owners

Because of the difficulty of tracing the ownership of kennel names when applied to dogs, the following lists a large number of kennel prefixes and suffixes together with names of their owner or owners. The first lists American Kennels, the second British Kennels. No attempt has been made to have these listings complete since many more kennels have existed than are listed here. However, the names given are believed to be representative of the breed and include a large number of the more successful kennels through the years. In many cases the kennels listed are no longer in operation.

American Kennels

Acton Hill	Mr. and Mrs. John Kemps
Al-Scot	Mr. and Mrs. Harry Johnston, Jr.
Am Anger	E. B. Jarvis
Anstamm	Mr. and Mrs. Anthony Stamm
Ardeecee	Mr. and Mrs. Irwin Czeskleba
Ardmore	Robert McKinven
Ayerscott	Mr. and Mrs. Albert C. Ayres
Balachan	Dr. and Mrs. T. Allen Kirk
Baleshare	Mr. and Mrs. R. Offutt
Balgay	Dr. and Mrs. Cecil Jelley
Ballantrae	Caswell Barrie
Barberry Knowe	Mr. and Mrs. Charles C. Stalter, now Miss Barbara Kingsbury
Barlae	William Prentice (Also used in Britain)
Ben Braggie	Fred Fraser (Canada)
Bentley	Prentice Talmadge
Blanart	Mrs. Blanche Reeg
Boglebrae	Henry D. Bixby
Bothkennar	Mr. and Mrs. Bryce Gillespie, later by Mr. and Mrs Gordon D. Campbell
Brandywine	Mrs. George Thomas
Braw Bricht	Mr. and Mrs. Donald D. Voorhees
Brawyn	Mr. and Mrs. Turk Humphrey
Briarcroft	Dr. F. W. Zimmerman
Camydnas	A. E. Cartwright
Camyscot	Mrs. J. G. Myers & Mrs. C. Davis
Cantray	Linda L. Catlin
Carmichael's	Mrs. Ruth C. Johnson
Carnation	E. H. Stuart
Castlecrag	Mr. and Mrs. W. L. Dunham
Cedar Pond	John Goudie
Clanranold	Ron and Lois Giese

Craigdarroch	Mrs. Jack Brazier
Crescent Hill	Mrs. Dorissa Barnes
Crissot	Miss Cornelia M. Crissey
Cy Ann	Cyrus K. Rickel
Deephaven	Theodore W. Bennett
Diehard	William McBain
Dunbar	Richard Hensel
Earlybird	W. T. Stern
Easter Ross	Mrs. John A. Munro
Edgerstoune	Mrs. Marion Eppley (formerly Mrs. John G. Winant)
Elscot	Mrs. Louise Elsworth
Fairworld	R. M. Cadwalader
Firebrand	John Sheehan
Frangan	Mrs. Frances Gannon
Friendship Farm	Mr. and Mrs. William Sheiburn
Fullivit	Mr. and Mrs. W. Sheldon Winans
Gaddiscot	Mrs. W. F. Wendell
Gaidoune	Miss Helen B. Gaither, Miss Barbara Z. Lundell
Gilwyn	Mr. and Mrs. G. Robinson
Glad-Mac	Mrs. W. M. Robertson
Glenafton	Elizabeth Hull
Glenby	Mrs. F. J. Russell
Glenlivet	Miss C. Reid
Glen Shiel	Mr. and Mrs. Bernard P. Howes
Glentadbar	Mrs. B. Dominski (Canada)
Goldfinder	Edward F. Maloney
Graecroft	Mrs. Charles Gray
Gren-Aery	Mrs. J. Eagle
Hampton Hill	Mr. and Mrs. Werner Josten
Haycliff	Mr. and Mrs. Harry Haylor
Heatherbelle	Mrs. M. Mellish (Canada)
Heatherlane	Mr. and Mrs. Nicholas Levandoski
Hibank	Mr. and Mrs. F. R. Newton
Highlander	Dr. and Mrs. Joseph A. Thomas
Hillcote	John Hillman
Hillwood	Mrs. Thomas W. Durant
Hil-Ray's	Mr. and Mrs. Raymond Bigelow
Hitofa	Frank Spierkerman
Jaudon	Mr. and Mrs. Ronald Barker
Jepeca	Mr. and Mrs. Charles H. Werber, Jr.
Kelti	Mrs. John V. Kelly
Kelscot	Mr. and Mrs. Joseph W. Kelly
Kenbrick	Mr. and Mrs. Kenneth Halloran
Kenjo	Mr. and Mrs. Kennan Glaser
Kildoran	Mr. and Mrs. E. M. Richardson (Canada)
Kinclaven	Mrs. Marie A. Stone
Kirk-Nor	Mrs. Judith Bonaiuto
Lady Alberta	Mrs. Vana Mapplebeck
Lealscot	Mrs. John McGilvray
Lochearn	Mr. and Mrs. Charles J. Costabell
Lynnscot	Mr. and Mrs. R. J. McLoughlin

Mac-Bur	Marguerite J. Fuller
MacLapin	Mr. and Mrs. Bart Lapin
Mac R	Mr. and Mrs. Keith P. Rogers
Mac's Welton	Mr. and Mrs. William Macauley
Marlorain	Miss Lorraine Davis and Miss Martha Melekov
Marlu	Mr. and Mrs. Maurice Pollak
Marymac	Dr. and Mrs. B. Kater McInnes
Medrick	Mrs. Medora Messinger
Merrie Oaks	Mrs. Edmund Mansure
Merriland	Mrs. M. Merrill
Middlemount	Bruce Webb
Mine Brook	Jock McOwan
Newcastle	James and Dr. C. C. Little
Nosegay	Dr. Fayette Ewing
'of Seaglen	R. C. E. Sharp (Canada)
Paisley Hill	Mr. and Mrs. Henry D. Israel
Philabeg	Dr. and Mrs. Merritt N. Pope
Poverty Hill	John F. Wright, Jr.
Raab Hill	Mrs. A. Marshall
Rampant	Mr. and Mrs. Seth Malby
Rannoch Dune	Mr. and Mrs. Frank Brumby
Rebellee	Miss J. Crosier (Canada)
Rebel Run	Dr. and Mrs. W. Stewart Carter
Red Gauntlet	Dr. and Mrs. Charles Lynch
Redoubts	Mr. and Mrs. Don Plott
Relgalf	Mrs. Flagler Matthews
Renaldo	Mr. and Mrs. James Reynolds (Canada)
Revran	Mrs. Richard Swatsley
Ruff-Me-Tuff	Jake & Nancy McCloskey
Sagette	Stewart Gettle
Sandbark	Miss Evelyn Sanders
Sandoone	Miss Betty Malinka
Sandown	Mrs. E. S. Woodward
Sandreg	Mr. and Mrs. John DeSaye
Scots Delight	Dorothy Morris
Scots Guard	Mrs. Richard Weaver
Scotsholme	Bert Hankinson
Sharonlane	Mr. and Mrs. Reason A. Krick
Shenscot	Mr. and Mrs. L. Bradford Branner
Shieling	Mr. and Mrs. T. Howard Snethen
Sonata	Mr. and Mrs. K. Lowman
Sporran	S. S. Van Dine
Stonehedge	Don Massaker and Thomas Natalini
Tavviscot	Mr. and Mrs. S. Valdes
Terriwall	Mr. and Mrs. Bengt Wallgren
Three Thistle	Alfred Mitchell
Tobermory	Mrs. George Cole (Marguerite Kirmse)
Todhill	Mr. and Mrs. Robert C. Graham
Tomarhon	Mr. and Mrs. T. Johnson
Vigal	Mr. and Mrs. H. Alvin McAleenan
Vimy Ridge	Clifford and Enid Hallmark

Ch. MacLapin Just A Sample, CDX had a successful career in conformation competition and in obedience. He was trained by Marc Lapin and is shown here qualifying for his CD degree. In addition to becoming a CDX he also earned the CD degree in Canada.

Diehard Fashion, owned by Diehard Kennels and handled by Phil Prentice, was BB at Westminster 1942 under Charles C. Stalter.

Ch. Mayson Morag, owned by Mr. and Mrs. John S. Gaskell, first recipient of the Singleton Memorial Trophy with which she is here posed.

Ch. Gaywyn Landmark, owned by Mr. and Mrs. John S. Gaskell, with the Club trophy he won for being England's top stud dog for 1978.

248

Walescot	Francis G. Lloyd
Wankie	Henry Brooks and Oliver Ames
Wayridge	Mr. and Mrs. Wayne Ridgley
Wee Ben	Mrs. Louise Benham
Wishing Well	Mrs. Florence Worcester
Woodhart	Mr. and Mrs. Heywood Hartley
Yankee Pride	Peter Babisch

British Kennels

Abertay	B. McMillam
Albourne	A. G. Cowley
Allascot	Miss D. Blackstone
Baldinny	Mrs. S. Grieve
Balgownie	A. Black
Bapton	J. Deane Willis
Bardene	W. Palethorpe
Barlae	William Prentice (also in the U.S.)
Bidfield	Miss R. Payne and Miss S. M. Harrold
Brio	Miss Jane Miller
Broadeaves	Miss D. M. White
Clynebury	H. Davies
Craig	Miss P. Drummond
Cumnoch	Miss B. Sedorski
Darmar	Mrs. M. Darroch
Desco	Mrs. L. J. Dewar
Desert	R. J. Gadsden
Dove Coat	Mrs. S. J. Corby & Mrs. E. I. Crowden
Eckersley	Miss M. Law
Eilburn	Mrs. M. Punton
Elbury	Mrs. Rees
Ems	W. L. McCandlish
Eros Scot	F. J. Backham
Farnock	Robert Houston
Gaisgill	Mrs. C. M. Cross
Gaywyn	Mr. and Mrs. H. F. Owen
Gillsie	W. Gill and J. McShane
Gillson	Mr. and Mrs. A. Gill
Glendoune	R. H. McGill
Glenecker	Mrs. M. A., Micklethwaite
Glenisla	Mr. and Mrs. A. M. Robb
Glenview	Mr. and Mrs. A. H. Gee
Gosmore	Mrs. A. S. Dallison
Gourock	Messrs. Mackie and McColl
Gregorach	Miss P. Drummond
Heather	Robert Chapman and sons
Inverdruie	Miss L. Vassilopulo
Jetscot	Mr. and Mrs. H. Smead
Jhelum	G. D. Lyell

249

Eng. Ch. Bramshire Brenda, owned by Ernest Joeresco.

Eng. Ch. Mayson Canasta, owned by Mr. and Mrs. John S. Gaskell.

Kennelgarth	Miss Betty Penn Bull
Laindon	H. R. B. Tweed
Mayson	Mr. and Mrs. J. S. Gaskell
Niddbank	J. R. and Mrs. K. M. Ross
Noonsun	Mrs. N. Holland
Ortley	Dr. C. Bremer
'of Ralc	Miss D. I. Thorpe
Penvale	J. Jeffs
Reanda	Mrs. E. Meyer
'of Rookes	John Sharpe
Rothesay	Andrew H. Lister
Ryeland	Mrs. S. A. Collins
Sandheys	Richard Lloyd
Scotia	Mrs. W. Barber
Stedplane	Mrs. E. Plane
Tadwick	Mrs. F. M. Sheppard
Tiddlymount	J. P. Dodgson
Triermain	Mrs. M. E. Bousfield
Turfield	T. W. L. Caspersz
Viewpark	Mr. and Mrs. A. Maclaren
Walnut	Sam Bamford
Walsing	Mr. and Mrs. W. M. Singleton
Wenbury	T. W. and Mrs. D. M. Randall
Woodmansey	H. Wright
Wychworth	H. Knowles
Wyrebury	W. Berry

The magic of Christmas, the innocence of childhood and the Scot's affinity for both enhance this delightful Edwin Megargee holiday illustration.

An Overview of
Today's Scottish Terrier

IN RETROSPECT, there are some important facts to survey which concern today's Scottish Terrier. The popularity of the breed reached its all-time peak in 1971 when 10,756 dogs were registered as compared with 6,430 in 1978. This decrease in registrations has caused a concurrent drop in show entries. The general situation is not believed to be based upon a lessening of interest in the breed but rather to the loss of a number of strong breeders through death with a reduction in breeding activity within a large segment of the fancy who find adequate help difficult to obtain. Of great importance too, is the progressive loss of the large kennel replete with private handler and staff, these have all but disappeared. Today, most breeders care for their own stock and a kennel of about ten adult dogs is considered better than average size as compared to from fifty to 100 dogs before World War II. Kennels of hard-haired, heavily-trimmed Terriers, such as, Scots, Wires, Welsh, or Airedales, require more time and effort than do untrimmed or scissored breeds. In today's hectic life, many newer fanciers have not learned this complex art well enough to be able to compete against those of greater proficiency. It is incumbent upon all who love the breed to master the art of trimming and conditioning so that the Scotsman is kept in the eye of the public, for once seen, it is only a matter of time before it will find a way into the heart of any dog lover.

These are not idle words; they mirror the beliefs of many students of the trends in popularity of the several breeds and they reflect some of the reasons for the growth or regression of interest among the recognized breeds. After all, dog shows have multiplied vastly during the past twenty years. Overall entries have sky-rocketed and the Scotsman should be enjoying a similar rise in support but it is not. It is the fancy's responsibility to improve the lot of the Scottish Terrier by offering greater support at the shows, improving the stock and making a concerted effort to enlist and train new owners and exhibitors. Truly, the Scotsman is a special breed whose virtues, rigid scrutiny defy, for as Francis Butler wrote more than 130 years ago:

> Small, rough and whiskery, and of sandy hue,
> Though, sometimes gray, and oft of dusky blue;*
> Clear, bright, inquisitive, sagacious eye,
> Mustachoid lip, with brows deep shaded by;
> Brave, hardy, vigilant and ever gay,
> First famed on Scotia's lofty hills they say;
> Kills fox and weasel, skunk, racoon, and cat,
> Rabbit or squirrel, hedgehog, mouse or rat;
> Onward he rushes, with impetuous ire,
> His wiry pelt dares bramble, bush, and briar,
> Through matter brakes he threads his thorny way,
> Digs in the earth or tempts the flood for prey;
> Not swift of limb, the fleeter game to trace,
> Of noxious vermin rids the house and store,
> Inspects each corner, searches every floor;
> When cunning Renard, pressed by boisterous hounds
> Rushes to earth, and thus the pack confounds,
> The valiant Scot assails him in his den,
> All gore begrimmed, he drags him forth again;
> His coarse exterior some may chance condemn,
> Others his blunt expression may condemn;
> Yet, none his virtues ever dare deny;
> His merits rigid scrutiny defy.

*The "dusky blue" color referred to suggests a Skye terrier cross that was not uncommon at the time.

Scottish Terrier Bibliography

The following lists books and articles that deal with the breed in whole or in part.

Ash, E. C. — *The Scottish Terrier*, 1936.
  Dogs, Their History and Development, 2 vol., 1927.
Ashmore, Marion — *Lost, Stolen or Strayed, 1931.*
Barrie, Caswell — *The New Scottish Terrier Standard, American Kennel Gazette*, March 1925 pp 20-22, 151.
Barton, F. T. — *Terriers, Their Points and Management*, 1907.
Bruette, Dr. William — *The Scottish Terrier*, 1934.
Buckley, Holland — *The Scottish Terrier*, 1918.
Caspersz, D. S. — *Scottish Terrier Pedigrees*, with supplements, 1930, 1934, 1951, 1962.
  What the Scottie Will Become, *American Kennel Gazette*, July 1931 pp 25-27, 119.
  The Scottish Terrier, 1938.
  The Scottish Terrier (Foyles), 1958.
  The Popular Scottish Terrier, 1956, 1962. Revised by Elizabeth Meyer, 1976.
Davies, C. J. — *The Scottish Terrier*, 1906.
Deu, Edna *et al.* — *Stars in the Doghouse* (Deephaven Kennels) *Country Life In America*, April 1939 pp 55, 109-110.

Elliott, K. (Della) *Notes on the Standard of the Scottish Terrier. 1976. A comparative analysis as viewed in books on the breed by Caspersz, Kirk and Marvin. Published in New South Wales.*

Ewing, Dr. Fayette— *The Book of the Scottish Terrier,* 1932 and subsequent ed.

Gabriel, Dorothy— *The Scottish Terrier,* 1928, 1936

Gray, D. J. Thomson— *The Dogs of Scotland,* 1887 and 1893 (Whinstone).

Green, James E.— *The Scottish Terrier and the Irish Terrier,* 1894.

Haynes, William— *Scottish and Irish Terriers,* 1912, 1925.

Johns, Rowland— *Our Friend the Scottish Terrier,* 1932.

Jones, A. F.— *American Kennel Gazette,* Ballantrae's Reasons for Success, March 1927 pp 13-17, 71; Hillwood Turns to the Scottie, Feb. 1932 pp 9-13; Bred by Science and Humanity (Sporran Kennels), July 1932 pp 7-11, 124; Vigal is Building Slowly, Dec. 1932 pp 24-28, 157; A Kennel without a Fault (Relgalf Kennels) July 1934 pp 7-11, 173; Why Braw Bricht's Aim is to Breed Scotties of Highest Quality, Feb. 1936 pp 12-15, 99; Championship, the Standard for Scotties of Miss Hull, March 1936 pp 11-14, 79; Raising Scotties that Win is Greatest Enjoyment to Owners of Barberry Knowe, July 1936 pp 13-16, 152; Scotties Started Relgalf on the Way to Fame, Aug. 1938 pp 27-31.

Kipling, Rudyard— *The Supplication of the Black Aberdeen,* 1931. *Thy Servant the Dog,* 1930.

Kirk, Dr. T. Allen— *American Scottish Terrier Champions' Pedigrees,* 1962. *This Is the Scottish Terrier,* 1966.

Kirmse, M.— A Derrydale Press book of etchings, mostly Scots, 1930.

Lucas, E. V.— *If Dogs Could Write,* 1929.

Marvin, John T.— *The Book of All Terriers,* 1964, includes breed chapter.

Matheson, Darley— *Terriers, 1962,* includes breed chapter.

Mason, Charles H.— *Our Prize Dogs,* 1888.

Maxtee, J.— *British Terriers,* 1909; *Scotch and Irish Terriers,* 1909, 1923.

McCandlish, W. L.— Chapter on the breed in *Dogs by Well Known Authorities,* 1906— *The Scottish Terrier,* 1909.

Megargee, Edwin S.— The Ideal Scottish Terrier, *American Kennel Gazette,* Jan. 1933 pp 17-20, 136.

Penn Bull, Betty— *Scottish Terrier Coats,* Re trimming the breed. n.d.

Robertson, James— *Historical Sketches of the Scottish Terrier,* 1899.

Scottish Terrier Club of America Yearbooks, 1948, 1959, 1961, 1965.

Scottish Terrier Club of England Yearbooks, various issues.

Smith, Croxton— *Terriers, Their Training, Working and Management,* 1937. Includes chapters on the breed by McCandlish.

Shields, G. O.— *The American Book on the Dog,* 1891. Includes chapter on the breed by John H. Naylor.

Stables, Dr. Gordon— *Our Friend the Dog,* © 1883.

Van Dine, S. S.— Crashing the Dog-Breeding Gate, *American Kennel Gazette,* Dec. 1930 pp 29-32, 166.
The Kennel Murder Case, 1932.

Watson, James— *The Dog Book,* 1906, 2 vol. includes much early comment on the breed in America.

There are many more books that contain chapters on the breed. Most are useful but the ones mentioned will offer the reader a complete resume of the important literature on the breed.

Dundee
Rascal
Sassy Lassie
Heather
Jere